P O E

DESCRIPTIVE OF

RURAL LIFE AND SCENERY

JOHN CLARE

ISBN: 978-1495421716

Table of Contents

SONGS & BALLADS

SONNETS

HELPSTONE

HAIL, humble Helpstone! where thy valleys spread,
And thy mean village lifts its lowly head;
Unknown to grandeur, and unknown to fame;
No minstrel boasting to advance thy name:
Unletter'd spot! unheard in poets' song;
Where bustling Labour drives the hours along;
Where dawning Genius never met the day;
Where useless Ignorance slumbers life away;
Unknown nor heeded, where, low Genius tries
Above the vulgar, and the vain, to rise.
   Mysterious Fate! who can on thee depend?
Thou opes' the hour, but hides' its doubtful end:
In Fancy's view the joys have long appear'd,
Where the glad heart by laughing plenty's cheer'd;
And Fancy's eyes as oft, as vainly, fill;
At first but doubtful, and as doubtful still.
So little birds, in winter's frost and snow,
Doom'd, like to me, want's keener frost to know;
Searching for food and "better life," in vain;
(Each hopeful track the yielding snows
retain;)
First on the ground each fairy dream pursue,
Though sought in vain; yet bent on higher view,
Still chirp, and hope, and wipe each glossy bill;
And undiscourag'd, undishearten'd still,
Hop on the snow-cloth'd bough, and chirp again,
Heedless of naked shade and frozen plain:
Till, like to me, these victims of the blast,
Each foolish, fruitless wish resign'd at last,
Are glad to seek the place from whence they went
And put up with distress, and be content.
   Hail, scenes obscure! so near and dear to me,
The church, the brook, the cottage, and the tree:
Still shall obscurity rehearse the song,
And hum your beauties as I stroll along.
Dear, native spot! which length of time endears;

The sweet retreat of twenty lingering years,
And, oh! those years of infancy the scene;
Those dear delights, where once they all have been;
Those golden days, long vanish'd from the plain;
Those sports, those pastimes, now belov'd in vain;
When happy youth in pleasure's circle ran,
Nor thought what pains awaited future man;
No other thought employing, or employ'd,
But how to add to happiness enjoy'd:
Each morning wak'd with hopes before unknown,
And eve, possessing, made each wish their own;
The day gone by left no pursuit undone,
Nor one vain wish, save that it went too soon;
Each sport, each pastime, ready at their call,
As soon as wanted they possess'd them all:
These joys, all known in happy infancy,
And all I ever knew, were spent in thee.
And who, but loves to view where these were past?
And who, that views, but loves them to the last?
Feels his heart warm to view his native place,
A fondness still those past delights to trace?
The vanish'd green to mourn, the spot to see
Where flourish'd many a bush and many a tree?
Where once the brook, for now the brook is gone,
O'er pebbles dimpling sweet went whimpering
on;
Oft on whose oaken plank I've wondering stood,
(That led a pathway o'er its gentle flood),
To see the beetles their wild mazes run,
With jetty jackets glittering in the sun:
So apt and ready at their reels they seem,
So true the dance is figur'd on the stream,
Such justness, such correctness they impart,
They seem as ready as if taught by art.
In those past days, for then I lov'd the shade,
How oft I've sigh'd at alterations made;
To see the woodman's cruel axe employ'd,
A tree beheaded, or a bush destroy'd:
Nay e'en a post, old standard, or a stone

Moss'd o'er by Age, and branded as her own,
Would in my mind a strong attachment gain,
A fond desire that there they might remain;
And all old favourites, fond Taste approves,
Griev'd me at heart to witness their removes.

Thou far fled pasture, long evanish'd scene!
Where nature's freedom spread the flow'ry green;
Where golden kingcups open'd into view;
Where silver daisies in profusion grew;
And, tottering, hid amidst those brighter gems,
Where silken grasses bent their tiny stems:
Where the pale lilac, mean and lowly, grew,
Courting in vain each gazer's heedless view;
While cowslips, sweetest flowers upon the plain,
Seemingly bow'd to shun the hand, in vain:
Where lowing oxen roam'd to feed at large,
And bleating there the shepherd's woolly charge,
Whose constant calls thy echoing valleys cheer'd,
Thy scenes adorn'd, and rural life endear'd;
No calls of hunger Pity's feelings wound,
'Twas wanton Plenty rais'd the joyful sound:
Thy grass in plenty gave the wish'd supply,
Ere sultry suns had wak'd the troubling fly;
Then blest retiring, by thy bounty fed,
They sought thy shades, and found an easy bed.

But now, alas! those scenes exist no more;
The pride of life with thee, like mine, is o'er,
Thy pleasing spots to which fond memory clings,
Sweet cooling shades, and soft refreshing springs.
And though Fate's pleas'd to lay their beauties by
In a dark corner of obscurity,
As fair and sweet they bloom'd thy plains among,
As bloom those Edens by the poets sung;
Now all laid waste by Desolation's hand,
Whose cursed weapons level half the land.
Oh! who could see my dear green willows fall,
What feeling heart, but dropt a tear for all?

Accursed Wealth! o'er-bounding human laws,
Of every evil thou remain'st the cause:
Victims of want, those wretches such as me,
Too truly lay their wretchedness to thee:
Thou art the bar that keeps from being fed,
And thine our loss of labour and of bread;
Thou art the cause that levels every tree,
And woods bow down to clear a way for thee.

Sweet Rest and Peace! ye dear, departed charms,
Which Industry once cherish'd in her arms;
When ease and plenty, known but now to few,
Were known to all, and labour had its due;
When Mirth and Toil, companions through the day,
Made labour light, and pass'd the hours away;
When Nature made the fields so dear to me,
Thin scattering many a bush and many a tree;
Where the Wood-Minstrel sweetly join'd among,
And cheer'd my needy toilings with a song;
Ye perish'd spots, adieu! ye ruin'd scenes,
Ye well known pastures, oft frequented greens!
Though now no more, fond Memory's pleasing pains,
Within her breast your every scene retains.
Scarce did a bush spread its romantic bower,
To shield the lazy shepherd from the shower;
Scarce did a tree befriend the chattering pye,
By lifting up its head so proud and high;
No, not a secret spot did then remain,
Throughout each spreading wood and winding plain,
But, in those days, my presence once possess'd,
The snail-horn searching, or the mossy nest.

Oh, happy Eden of those golden years
Which memory cherishes, and use endears,
Thou dear, beloved spot! may it be thine
To add a comfort to my life's decline,
When this vain world and I have nearly done,
And Time's drain'd glass has little left to run.
When all the hopes, that charm'd me once, are o'er,

To warm my soul in extacy no more,
By disappointments prov'd a foolish cheat,
Each ending bitter, and beginning sweet;
When weary Age the grave, a rescue, seeks,
And prints its image on my wrinkled cheeks,—
Those charms of youth, that I again may see,
May it be mine to meet my end in thee;
And, as reward for all my troubles past,
Find one hope true—to die at home at last!

ADDRESS TO A LARK, SINGING IN WINTER

AY, little Larky! what's the reason,
Singing thus in winter season?
Nothing, surely, can be pleasing
  To make thee sing;
For I see nought but cold and freezing,
  And feel its sting.

Perhaps, all done with silent mourning,
Thou think'st that Summer is returning,
And this the last, cold, frosty morning,
  To chill thy breast;
If so, I pity thy discerning:
  And so I've guess'd.
Poor, little Songster! vainly cheated;
Stay, leave thy singing uncompleted;
Drop where thou wast beforehand seated,
  In thy warm nest;
Nor let vain wishes be repeated,
  But sit at rest.

'Tis Winter; let the cold content thee:
Wish after nothing till its sent thee,
For disappointments will torment thee,
Which will be thine:
I know it well, for I've had plenty
Misfortunes mine.

Advice, sweet Warbler! don't despise it:
None knows what's what, but he that tries it;
And then he well knows how to prize it,
    And so do I:
Thy case, with mine I sympathise it,
    With many a sigh.

Vain Hope! of thee I've had my portion;
Mere flimsy cobweb! changing ocean!
That flits the scene at every motion,
    And still eggs on,
With sweeter view, and stronger notion
    To dwell upon:—

Yes, I've dwelt long on idle fancies,
Strange and uncommon as romances,
On future luck my noddle dances,
    What I would be;
But, ah! when future time advances,
    All's blank to me.

Now twenty years I've pack'd behind me,
Since Hope's deluding tongue inclin'd me
To fuss myself. But, Warbler, mind me,
    It's all a sham;
And twenty more's as like to find me
    Just as I am.

I'm poor enough, there's plenty knows it;
Obscure; how dull, my scribbling shews it:
Then sure 'twas madness to suppose it,
    What I was at,
To gain preferment!—there I'll close it:
    So mum for that.

Let mine, sweet Bird, then be a warning:
Advice, in season, don't be scorning;
But wait till Spring's first days are dawning
    To glad and cheer thee;

And then, sweet Minstrel of the morning,
   I'd wish to hear thee.

THE FATE OF AMY: A TALE

BENEATH a sheltering wood's warm side,
   Where many a tree expands
Its branches o'er the neighbouring brook,
   A ruin'd cottage stands:
Though now left desolate, and lost
   Its origin, and all;
Owls hooting from the roofless walls,
   Rejoicing in its fall;

A time was once, remembrance knows,
   Though now the time's gone by,
When that was seen to flourish gay,
   And pleasing to the eye.
On that same ground the brambles hide,
   And stinking weeds o'er-run,
An orchard bent its golden boughs,
   And redden'd in the sun.

Yon nettles where they're left to spread,
   There once a garden smil'd;
And lovely was the spot to view,
   Though now so lost and wild:

And where the sickly elder loves
   To top the mouldering wall;
And ivy's kind encroaching care
   Delays the tottering fall;

There once a mother's only joy,
   A daughter lovely, fair,
As ever bloom'd beneath the sun,
   Was nurs'd and cherish'd there.
The cottage then was known around;
   The neighbouring village swains

Would often wander by to view
  That charmer of the plains.

Where softest blush of roses wild,
  And hawthorn's fairest blow,
But meanly serve to paint her cheek,
  And bosom's rival snow;
The loveliest blossom of the plains,
  The artless Amy prov'd;
In nature's sweetest charms adorn'd,
  Those charms by all belov'd.

Sweet Innocence! the beauty's thine
  That every bosom warms:
Fair as she was, she liv'd alone
  A stranger to her charms.
Unmov'd the praise of swains she heard,
  Nor proud at their despair;
But thought they scoff'd her when they prais'd;
  And knew not she was fair.

Nor did she for the joys of youth
  Forsake her mother's side,
Who then by age and pain infirm'd,
  On her for help relied.

No tenderer mother to a child
  Throughout the world could be;
And, in return, no daughter prov'd
  More dutiful than she.

The pains of age she sympathiz'd,
  And sooth'd, and wish'd to share:
In short, the aged, helpless dame
  Was Amy's only care.

But age had pains, and they were all:
  Life's cares they little knew;
Its billows ne'er encompass'd them,

They waded smoothly through.

The tender father, now no more,
  Did for them both provide;
The wealth his industry had gain'd,
  All wants to come supplied.

Kind heaven upon their labours smil'd;
  Industry gave increase;
The cottage was contentment's own
  Abode of health and peace.

Alas! the tongue of Fate is seal'd,
  And kept for ever dumb:
To-morrow's met with blinded eyes;
  We know not what's to come.

Blithe as the lark, as crickets gay
  That chirrup'd on the hearth,
This Sun of Beauty's time was spent
  In inoffensive mirth.

Meek as the lambs that throng'd her door,
  As innocent as they,
Her hours pass'd on, and charms improv'd
  With each succeeding day.

So, smiling on the sunny plain,
  The lovely daisies blow,
Unconscious of the careless foot
  That lays their beauty low.

So blooms the lily of the vale;
  (Ye beauties, oh, be wise!)
Untimely blasts o'ertake its bloom,
  It withers, and it dies.

The humble cottage lonely stood
  Far from the neighbouring vill;

Its church, that topp'd the willow groves,
  Lay far upon the hill;

Which made all company desir'd,
  And welcome to the dame:
And oft to tell the village news,
  The neighbouring gossips came.

Young Edward mingled with the rest:
  An artful swain was he,
Who laugh'd, and told his merry jests;
  For custom made him free:

And oft with Amy toy'd and play'd,
  While, harmless as the dove,
Her artless, unsuspecting heart
  But little thought of love.

But frequent visits gain'd esteem,
  Each time of longer stay;
And custom did his name endear:—
  He stole her heart away.

So fairest flowers adorn the wild;
  And, most endanger'd, stand
The soonest seen;—a certain prey
  To some destroying hand.

Her choice was fix'd on him alone;
  The rest but vainly strove:
And worse than all the rest is he;
  But blind the eyes of love.

Of him full many a maid complain'd
  The lover of an hour,
That, like the ever changing bee,
  Sipp'd sweets from every flower.
Alas! those slighted pains are small,
  If all such maidens know;

But she was fair, and he design'd
  To work her further woe.

Her innocence his bosom fir'd,
  So long'd to be enjoy'd;
And he, to gain his wish'd-for ends,
  Each subtle art employ'd.

Ah! he employ'd his subtle arts,
  Alas, too sad to tell;
The winning ways which he employ'd,
  Succeeded but too well.

So artless, innocent, and young,
  So ready to believe;
A stranger to the world was she,
  And easy to deceive.

Ah! now farewel to beauty's boast,
  Charms so admir'd before;
Now innocence has lost its sweets,
  Her beauties bloom no more.

The flowers, the sultry Summer kills,
  Spring's milder suns restore;
But Innocence, that fickle charm,
  Blooms once, and blooms no more.

The swains who lov'd, no more admire,
  Their hearts no beauty warms;
And maidens triumph in her fall,
  That envied once her charms.

Lost was that sweet simplicity;
  Her eye's bright lustre fled;
And o'er her cheeks, where roses bloom'd,
  A sickly paleness spread.

So fades the flower before its time,

Where canker-worms assail;
So droops the bud upon its stem,
   Beneath the sickly gale.

The mother saw the sudden change,
   Where health so lately smil'd;
Too much—and, oh! suspecting more,—
   Grew anxious for her child.

And all the kindness in her power
   The tender mother shows;
In hopes such kindly means would make
   Her fearless to disclose.

And oft she hinted, if a crime,
   Through ignorance beguil'd—
Not to conceal the crime in fear,
   For none should wrong her child.

Or, if the rose that left her cheek
   Was banish'd by disease,
"Fear God, my child!" she oft would say,
   "And you may hope for ease."

And still she pray'd, and still had hopes
   There was no injury done;
And still advis'd the ruin'd girl
   The world's deceit to shun.

And many a cautionary tale
   Of hapless maiden's fate,
From trusting man, to warn her, told;
   But told, alas! too late.

A tender mother's painful cares
   In vain the loss supply;
The wide-mouth'd world, its sport and scorn
   Than meet, she'd sooner die.

Advice but aggravated woe;
  And ease, an empty sound;
No one could ease the pains she felt,
  But he who gave the wound.

And he, wild youth, had left her now,
  Unfeeling as the stone:
Fair maids, beware, lest careless ways
  Make Amy's fate your own.

Ill-fated girl! too late she found,
  As but too many find,
False Edward's love as light as down,
  And vows as fleet as wind.

But one hope's left, and that she sought,
  To hide approaching shame;
And Pity, while she drops a tear,
  Forbears the rest to name.

The widow'd mother, though so old,
  And ready to depart,
Was not ordain'd to live her time;
  The sad news broke her heart.

Borne down beneath a weight of years,
  And all the pains they gave,
But little added weight requir'd
  To crush her in the grave.

The strong oak braves the rudest wind;
  While, to the breeze, as well
The sickly, aged willow falls,—
  And so the mother fell.

Beside the pool the willow bends,
  The dew-bent daisy weeps;
And where the turfy hillock swells,
  The luckless Amy sleeps.

EVENING

NOW grey-ey'd hazy Eve's begun
  To shed her balmy dew,
Insects no longer fear the sun,
  But come in open view.

Now buzzing, with unwelcome din,
  The heedless beetle bangs
Against the cow-boy's dinner-tin,
  That o'er his shoulder hangs.

And on he keeps in heedless pat,
  Till, quite enrag'd, the boy
Pulls off his weather-beaten hat,
  Resolving to destroy.

Yet thoughtless that he wrongs the clown,
  By blows he'll not be driven,
But buzzes on, till batter'd down
  For unmeant injury given.

Now from each hedge-row fearless peep
  The slowly-pacing snails,
Betraying their meand'ring creep,
  In silver-slimy trails.

The dew-worms too in couples start,
  But leave their holes in fear;
For in a moment they will part,
  If aught approaches near.

The owls mope out, and scouting bats
  Begin their giddy round;
While countless swarms of dancing gnats
  Each water pudge surround.

And 'side yon pool, as smooth as glass,

Reflecting every cloud,
Securely hid among the grass,
    The crickets chirrup loud.

That rural call, "*Come mulls! come mulls!*"
    From distant pasture-grounds,
All noises now to silence lulls,
    In soft and ushering sounds;

While echoes weak, from hill to hill
    Their dying sounds deplore,
That whimper faint and fainter still,
    Till they are heard no more.

The breezes, once so cool and brief,
    At Eve's approach all died;
None's left to make the aspen leaf
    Twirl up its hoary side.

But breezes all are useless now;
    The hazy dun, that spreads
Her moist'ning dew on every bough,
    Sufficient coolness sheds.

The flowers, reviving from the ground,
    Perk up again and peep,
While many different tribes around
    Are shutting up to sleep.

Now let me, hid in cultur'd plain,
    Pursue my evening walk,
Where each way beats the nodding grain,
    Aside the narrow balk;

While fairy visions intervene,
    Creating dread surprize,
From distant objects dimly seen,
    That catch the doubtful eyes.

And fairies now, no doubt, unseen,
  In silent revels sup;
With dew-drop bumpers toast their queen,
  From crow-flower's golden cup.

Although about these tiny things
  Folks make so much ado;
I never heed the darksome rings,
  Where they are said to go:

But Superstition still deceives;
  And fairies still prevail;
While stooping Genius e'en believes
  The customary tale.

Oh, loveliest time! oh, sweetest hours
  The musing soul can find!
Now, Evening, let thy soothing powers
  At freedom fill the mind.

WHAT IS LIFE?

AND what is Life?—An hour-glass on the run,
A mist retreating from the morning sun,
  A busy, bustling, still repeated dream.—
Its length?—A minute's pause, a moment's thought.
  And happiness?—A bubble on the stream,
That in the act of seizing shrinks to nought.

What is vain Hope?—The puffing gale of morn,
  That of its charms divests the dewy lawn,
And robs each flow'ret of its gem,—and dies;
  A cobweb hiding disappointment's thorn,
Which stings more keenly through the thin disguise.

—And thou, O Trouble?—nothing can suppose,
(And sure the power of wisdom only knows,)
  What need requireth thee:
So free and liberal as thy bounty flows,

Some necessary cause must surely be.
But disappointments, pains, and every woe
    Devoted wretches feel,
The universal plagues of life below,
    Are mysteries still 'neath Fate's unbroken seal.

And what is Death? is still the cause unfound?
That dark, mysterious name of horrid sound?—
    A long and lingering sleep, the weary crave.
And Peace? where can its happiness abound?—
    Nowhere at all, save heaven, and the grave.

Then what is Life?—When stripp'd of its disguise,
    A thing to be desir'd it cannot be;
Since every thing that meets our foolish eyes
    Gives proof sufficient of its vanity.
'Tis but a trial all must undergo;
    To teach unthankful mortals how to prize
That happiness vain man's denied to know,
    Until he's call'd to claim it in the skies.

ON A LOST GREYHOUND LYING ON THE SNOW

AH, thou poor, neglected hound!
    Now thou'st done with catching hares,
Thou mayst lie upon the ground,
    Lost, for what thy master cares.

To see thee lie, it makes me sigh:
    A proud, hard hearted man!
But men, we know, like dogs may go,
    When they've done all they can.

And thus, from witnessing thy fate,
    Thoughtful reflection wakes;
Though thou'rt a dog, with grief I say't,
    Poor man thy fare partakes:
Like thee, lost whelp, the poor man's help,

Erewhile so much desir'd,
Now harvest's got, is wanted not,
  Or little is requir'd.

So now, the overplus will be
  As useless negroes, all
Turn'd in the bitter blast, like thee
  Mere cumber-grounds, to fall:
But this reward, for toil so hard,
  Is sure to meet return
From Him, whose ear is always near,
  When the oppressed mourn.

For dogs, as men, are equally
  A link of Nature's chain,
Form'd by that hand that formed me,
  Which formeth nought in vain.
All life contains, as 'twere by chains,
  From Him still perfect are;
Nor does He think the meanest link
  Unworthy of His care.

So let us both on Him rely,
  And He'll for us provide;
Find us a shelter warm and dry,
  And every thing beside.

And while fools, void of sense, deride
  My tenderness to thee;
I'll take thee home, from whence I've come:
  So rise, and gang with me.

Poor, patient thing! he seems to hear
  And know what I have said;
He wags his tail, and ventures near,
  And bows his mournful head.
Thou'rt welcome: come! and though thou'rt dumb,
  Thy silence speaks thy pains;
So with me start, to share a part,

While I have aught remains.

A REFLECTION IN AUTUMN

Now Autumn's come, adieu the pleasing greens,
  The charming landscape, and the flow'ry plain!
All have deserted from these motley scenes,
  With blighted yellow ting'd, and russet stain.

Though Desolation seems to triumph here,
  Yet this is Spring to what we still shall find:
The trees must all in nakedness appear,
  'Reft of their foliage by the blustry wind.

Just so 'twill fare with me in Autumn's Life;
  Just so I'd wish: but may the trunk and all
Die with the leaves; nor taste that wintry strife,
  When sorrows urge, and fear impedes the fall.

4

THE ROBIN

Now the snow hides the ground, little birds leave the wood,
And fly to the cottage to beg for their food;
While the Robin, domestic, more tame than the rest,
With its wings drooping down, and its feathers undrest,
Comes close to our windows, as much as to say,
"I would venture in, if I could find a way:
I'm starv'd, and I want to get out of the cold;
Oh! make me a passage, and think me not bold."
Ah, poor little creature! thy visits reveal
Complaints such as these, to the heart that can
feel:
Nor shall such complainings be urged in vain;
I'll make thee a hole, if I take out a pane.
Come in, and a welcome reception thou'lt find:
I keep no grimalkin to murder inclin'd.
But oh, little Robin! be careful to shun

That house, where the peasant makes use of a gun;
For if thou but taste of the seed he has strew'd,
Thy life as a ransom must pay for the food:
His aim is unerring, his heart is as hard;
And thy race, though so harmless, he'll never regard.
Distinction with him, boy, is nothing at all;
Both the Wren, and the Robin, with Sparrows must fall.
For his soul (though he outwardly looks like a man,)
Is in nature a wolf of the Apennine clan;
Like them his whole study is bent on his prey:
Then be careful, and shun what is meant to betray.
Come, come to my cottage; and thou shalt be free
To perch on my finger, and sit on my knee:
Thou shalt eat of the crumbles of bread to thy fill,
And have leisure to clean both thy feathers and bill.
Then come, little Robin! and never believe
Such warm invitations are meant to deceive:
In duty I'm bound to show mercy on thee,
Since God don't deny it to sinners like me.

EPIGRAM

FOR fools that would wish to seem learned and wise,
    This receipt a wise man did bequeath;—
"Let 'em have the free use of their ears and their eyes;
    "But their tongue," says he, "tie to their teeth."

ADDRESS TO PLENTY, IN WINTER

O THOU bliss! to riches known,
Stranger to the poor alone;
Giving most where none's requir'd,
Leaving none where most's desir'd;
Who, sworn friend to miser, keeps'
Adding to his useless heaps

Gifts on gifts, profusely stor'd,
Till thousands swell the mouldy hoard:
While poor, shatter'd Poverty,
To advantage seen in me,
With his rags, his wants, and pain,
Waking pity but in vain,
Bowing, cringing at thy side,
Begs his mite, and is denied.
O, thou Blessing! let not me
Tell, as vain, my wants to thee;
Thou, by name of Plenty stil'd,
Fortune's heir, her favourite child.
'Tis a maxim—hunger feed,
Give the needy when they need;
He, whom all profess to serve,
The same maxim did observe:
Their obedience here, how well,
Modern times will plainly tell.
Hear my wants, nor deem me bold,
Not without occasion told:
Hear one wish; nor fail to give;
Use me well, and bid me live.

'Tis not great, what I solicit;
Was it more, thou couldst not miss it:
Now the cutting Winter's come,
'Tis but just to find a home,
In some shelter, dry and warm,
That will shield me from the storm.
Toiling in the naked fields,
Where no bush a shelter yields,
Needy Labour dithering stands,
Beats and blows his numbing hands;
And upon the crumping snows
Stamps, in vain, to warm his toes.
Leaves are fled, that once had power
To resist a summer shower;
And the wind so piercing blows,
Winnowing small the drifting snows,

27

The summer shade of loaded bough
Could vainly boast a shelter now:
Piercing snows so searching fall,
They sift a passage through them all.
Though all's vain to keep him warm,
Poverty must brave the storm.
Friendship none, its aid to lend:
Health alone his only friend;
Granting leave to live in pain,
Giving strength to toil in vain;
To be, while winter's horrors last,
The sport of every pelting blast.

Oh, sad sons of Poverty!
Victims doom'd to misery;
Who can paint what pain prevails
O'er that heart which Want assails?
Modest Shame the pain conceals:
No one knows, but he who feels.
Oh, thou charm which Plenty crowns,
Fortune! smile, now Winter frowns:
Cast around a pitying eye;
Feed the hungry, ere they die.
Think, oh! think upon the poor,
Nor against them shut thy door:
Freely let thy bounty flow,
On the sons of Want and Woe.

Hills and dales no more are seen
In their dress of pleasing green;
Summer's robes are all thrown by,
For the clothing of the sky;
Snows on snows in heaps combine,
Hillocks, rais'd as mountains, shine,
And at distance rising proud,
Each appears a fleecy cloud.
Plenty! now thy gifts bestow;
Exit bid to every woe:
Take me in, shut out the blast,

Make the doors and windows fast;
Place me in some corner, where,
Lolling in an elbow chair,
Happy, blest to my desire,
I may find a rouzing fire;
While in chimney-corner nigh,
Coal, or wood, a fresh supply,
Ready stands for laying on,
Soon as t'other's burnt and gone.
Now and then, as taste decreed,
In a book a page I'd read;
And, inquiry to amuse,
Peep at something in the news;
See who's married, and who's dead,
And who, through bankrupt, beg their bread:
While on hob, or table nigh,
Just to drink before I'm dry,
A pitcher at my side should stand,
With the barrel nigh at hand,
Always ready as I will'd,
When 'twas empty, to be fill'd;
And, to be possess'd of all,
A corner cupboard in the wall,
With store of victuals lin'd complete,
That when hungry I might eat.
Then would I, in Plenty's lap,
For the first time take a nap;
Falling back in easy lair,
Sweetly slumb'ring in my chair;
With no reflective thoughts to wake
Pains that cause my heart to ache,
Of contracted debts, long made,
In no prospect to be paid;
And, to Want, sad news severe,
Of provisions getting dear:
While the Winter, shocking sight,
Constant freezes day and night,
Deep and deeper falls the snow,
Labour's slack, and wages low.

These, and more, the poor can tell,
Known, alas, by them too well,
Plenty! oh, if blest by thee,
Never more should trouble me.
Hours and weeks will sweetly glide,
Soft and smooth as flows the tide,
Where no stones or choaking grass
Force a curve ere it can pass:
And as happy, and as blest,
As beasts drop them down to rest,
When in pastures, at their will,
 They have roam'd and eat their fill;
Soft as nights in summer creep,
So should I then fall asleep;
While sweet visions of delight,
So enchanting to the sight,
Sweetly swimming o'er my eyes,
Would sink me into extacies.
Nor would Pleasure's dreams once more,
As they oft have done before,
Cause be to create a pain,
When I woke, to find them vain:
Bitter past, the present sweet,
Would my happiness complete.
Oh! how easy should I lie,
With the fire up-blazing high,
(Summer's artificial bloom,)
That like an oven keeps the room,
Or lovely May, as mild and warm:
While, without, the raging storm
Is roaring in the chimney-top,
In no likelihood to drop;
And the witchen-branches nigh,
O'er my snug box towering high,
That sweet shelter'd stands beneath,
In convulsive eddies wreathe.
Then while, tyrant-like, the storm
Takes delight in doing harm,
Down before him crushing all,

Till his weapons useless fall;
And as in oppression proud
Peal his howlings long and loud,
While the clouds, with horrid sweep,
Give (as suits a tyrant's trade)
The sun a minute's leave to peep,
To smile upon the ruins made;
And to make complete the blast,
While the hail comes hard and fast,
Rattling loud against the glass;
And the snowy sleets, that pass,
Driving up in heaps remain
Close adhering to the pane,
Stop the light, and spread a gloom,
Suiting sleep, around the room:—
Oh, how blest 'mid these alarms,
I should bask in Fortune's arms,
Who, defying every frown,
Hugs me on her downy breast,
Bids my head lie easy down,
And on Winter's ruins rest.
So upon the troubled sea,
Emblematic simile,
Birds are known to sit secure,
While the billows roar and rave,
Slumbering in their safety sure,
Rock'd to sleep upon the wave.
So would I still slumber on,
Till hour-telling clocks had gone,
And, from the contracted day,
One or more had click'd away.
Then with sitting wearied out,
I for change's sake, no doubt,
Just might wish to leave my seat,
And, to exercise my feet,
Make a journey to the door,
Put my nose out, but no more:
There to village taste agree;
Mark how times are like to be;

How the weather's getting on;
Peep in ruts where carts have gone;
Or, by stones, a sturdy stroke,
View the hole the boys have broke,
Crizzling, still inclin'd to freeze;—
And the rime upon the trees.
Then, to pause on ills to come,
Just look upward on the gloom;
See fresh storms approaching fast,
View them busy in the air,
Boiling up the brewing blast,
Still fresh horrors scheming there.
Black and dismal, rising high,
 From the north they fright the eye:
Pregnant with a thousand storms,
Huddled in their icy arms,
Heavy hovering as they come,
Some as mountains seem—and some
Jagg'd as craggy rocks appear
Dismally advancing near:
Fancy, at the cumbrous sight,
Chills and shudders with affright,
Fearing lest the air, in vain,
Strives her station to maintain,
And wearied, yielding to the skies,
The world beneath in ruin lies.
So may Fancy think and feign;
Fancy oft imagines vain:
Nature's laws, by wisdom penn'd,
Mortals cannot comprehend;
Power almighty Being gave,
Endless Mercy stoops to save;
Causes, hid from mortals' sight,
Prove "whatever is, is right."
   Then to look again below,
Labour's former life I'd view,
Who, still beating through the snow,
Spite of storms their toils pursue,
Forc'd out by sad Necessity,

That sad fiend that forces me.
Troubles, then no more my own,
Which I but too long had known,
Might create a care, a pain;
Then I'd seek my joys again:
Pile the fire up, fetch a drink,
Then sit down again and think;
Pause on all my sorrows past,
Think how many a bitter blast,
When it snow'd, and hail'd, and blew,
I have toil'd and batter'd through.
Then to ease reflective pain,
To my sports I'd fall again,
Till the clock had counted ten;
When I'd seek my downy bed,
Easy, happy, and well fed.

Then might peep the morn, in vain,
Through the rimy misted pane;
Then might bawl the restless cock,
And the loud-tongued village clock;
And the flail might lump away,
Waking soon the dreary day:
They should never waken me,
Independent, blest, and free;
Nor, as usual, make me start,
Yawning sigh with heavy heart,
Loth to ope my sleepy eyes,
Weary still, in pain to rise,
With aching bones and heavy head,
Worse than when I went to bed.
With nothing then to raise a sigh,
Oh, how happy should I lie
Till the clock was eight, or more,
Then proceed as heretofore.
Best of blessings! sweetest charm!
Boon these wishes while they're warm;
My fairy visions ne'er despise;
As reason thinks, thou realize:

Depress'd with want and poverty,
I sink, I fall, denied by thee.

THE FOUNTAIN

HER dusky mantle Eve had spread;
The west sky glower'd with copper red;
Sun bid "good night," and slove to bed,
   'Hind black cloud's mimick'd mountain;
When weary from my toil I sped,
   To seek the purling fountain.

Labour had gi'en it up for good,
Save swains their folds that beetling stood,
While Echo, list'ning in the wood,
   Each knock kept 'stinctly counting;
The Moon just peep'd her horned hood,
   Faint glimmering in the fountain.

Ye gently dimpled, curling streams,
Rilling as smooth as summer-dreams,
Ill pair'd to yours Life's current seems,
   When Hope, rude cataracts mounting,
Bursts cheated into vain extremes,
   Far from the peaceful fountain.

I'd just streak'd down, and with a swish
Whang'd off my hat soak'd like a fish,
When 'bove what heart could think or wish—
   For chance there's no accounting—
A sweet lass came with wooden dish,
   And dipt it in the fountain.
I've often found a rural charm
In pastoral song my heart to warm,
But, faith, her beauties gave alarm,
   'Bove all I'd seen surmounting;
And when to the spring she stretch'd her arm,
   My heart chill'd in the fountain.

Simple, 'witching, artless maid,
So modestly she offer'd aid,
"And will you please to drink?" she said;
  My pulse beat past the counting;
Oh! Innocence such charms display'd,
  I can't forget the fountain.

Ere, lonely, home she 'gan proceed,
I said—what's secrecy indeed,
And offer'd company as need,
  The moon was highly mounting;
And still her charms—I'd scorn the deed—
  Were pure as was the fountain.

Ye leaning Palms, that seem to look
Pleas'd o'er your image in the brook,
Ye Ashes, harbouring pye and rook,
  Your shady boughs be mounting;
Ye Muses, leave Castalia's nook,
  And sacred make the fountain.

TO AN INSIGNIFICANT FLOWER, OBSCURELY BLOOMING IN A LONELY WILD

AND though thou seem'st a weedling wild,
  Wild and neglected like to me,
Thou still art dear to Nature's child,
  And I will stoop to notice thee.

For oft, like thee, in wild retreat,
  Array'd in humble garb like thee,
There's many a seeming weed proves sweet,
  As sweet as garden-flowers can be.
And, like to thee, each seeming weed
  Flowers unregarded; like to thee,
Without improvement, runs to seed,
  Wild and neglected like to me.

And, like to thee, when Beauty's cloth'd
  In lowly raiment like to thee,
Disdainful Pride, by Beauty loath'd,
  No beauties there can ever see.

For, like to thee, my Emma blows,
  A flower like thee I dearly prize;
And, like to thee, her humble clothes
  Hide every charm from prouder eyes.

But though, like thee, a lowly flower,
  If fancied by a polish'd eye,
She soon would bloom beyond my power,
  The finest flower beneath the sky.

And, like to thee, lives many a swain
  With genius blest; but, like to thee,
So humble, lowly, mean, and plain,
  No one will notice them,—or me.

So, like to thee, they live unknown,
  Wild weeds obscure; and, like to thee,
Their sweets are sweet to them alone:
  The only pleasure known to me.

Yet when I'm dead, let's hope I have
  Some friend in store, as I'm to thee,
That will find out my lowly grave,
  And heave a sigh to notice me.

ELEGY ON THE RUINS OF PICKWORTH, RUTLANDSHIRE, HASTILY COMPOSED, AND WRITTEN WITH A PENCIL ON THE SPOT

THESE buried ruins, now in dust forgot,
   These heaps of stone the only remnants seen,—
"The Old Foundations" still they call the spot,
   Which plainly tells inquiry what has been—

A time was once, though now the nettle grows
   In triumph o'er each heap that swells the ground,
When they, in buildings pil'd, a Village rose,
   With here a cot, and there a garden crown'd.

And here while Grandeur, with unequal share,
   Perhaps maintain'd its idleness and pride,
Industry's cottage rose contented there,
   With scarce so much as wants of life supplied.

Mysterious cause! still more mysterious plann'd;
   (Although undoubtedly the will of Heaven:)
To think what careless and unequal hand
   Metes out each portion that to man is given.

While vain Extravagance, for one alone,
   Claims half the land his grandeur to maintain;
What thousands, not a rood to call their own,
   Like me but labour for support in vain!

Here we see Luxury surfeit with excess;
   There Want, bewailing, beg from door to door,
Still meeting sorrow where he meets success,
   By lengthening Life that liv'd in vain before.

Almighty Power!—but why do I repine,
   Or vainly live thy goodness to distrust?
Since Reason rules each provident design,
   Whatever is must certainly be just.

Ye scenes of desolation spread around,
  Prosperity to you did once belong;
And, doubtless, where these brambles claim the ground,
  The glass once flow'd to hail the ranting song.

The ale-house here might stand, each hamlet's boast;
  And here, where elder rich from ruin grows,
The tempting sign—but what was once is lost;
Who would be proud of what this world bestows?

How Contemplation mourns their lost decay,
  To view their pride laid level with the ground;
To see, where Labour clears the soil away,
  What fragments of mortality abound.

There's not a rood of land demands our toil,
  There's not a foot of ground we daily tread,
But gains increase from time's devouring spoil,
  But holds some fragment of the human dead.

The very Food, which for support we crave,
  Claims for its share an equal portion too;
The dust of many a long-forgotten grave
  Serves to manure the soil from whence it grew.

Since first these ruins fell, how chang'd the scene!
  What busy, bustling mortals, now unknown,
Have come and gone, as tho' there nought had been,
  Since first Oblivion call'd the spot her own.

Ye busy, bustling mortals, known before,
  Of what you've done, where went, or what you see,
Of what your hopes attain'd to, (now no more,)
  For everlasting lies a mystery.

Like yours, awaits for me that common lot;
  'Tis mine to be of every hope bereft:
A few more years and I shall be forgot,
  And not a vestige of my memory left.

NOON

All how silent and how still;
Nothing heard but yonder mill:
While the dazzled eye surveys
All around a liquid blaze;
And amid the scorching gleams,
If we earnest look, it seems
As if crooked bits of glass
Seem'd repeatedly to pass.
Oh, for a puffing breeze to blow!
But breezes are all strangers now:
Not a twig is seen to shake,
Nor the smallest bent to quake;
From the river's muddy side
Not a curve is seen to glide;
And no longer on the stream
Watching lies the silver bream,
Forcing, from repeated springs,
"Verges in successive rings."
Bees are faint, and cease to hum;
Birds are overpower'd and dumb.
Rural voices all are mute,
Tuneless lie the pipe and flute:
Shepherds, with their panting sheep,
In the swaliest corner creep;
And from the tormenting heat
All are wishing to retreat.
Huddled up in grass and flowers,
Mowers wait for cooler hours;
And the cow-boy seeks the sedge,
Ramping in the woodland hedge,
While his cattle o'er the vales
Scamper, with uplifted tails;
Others not so wild and mad,
That can better bear the gad,
Underneath the hedge-row lunge,
Or, if nigh, in waters plunge.
Oh! to see how flowers are took,

How it grieves me when I look:
Ragged-robins, once so pink,
Now are turn'd as black as ink,
And the leaves, being scorch'd so much,
Even crumble at the touch;
Drowking lies the meadow-sweet,
Flopping down beneath one's feet:
While to all the flowers that blow,
If in open air they grow,
Th' injurious deed alike is done
By the hot relentless sun.
E'en the dew is parched up
From the teasel's jointed cup:
O poor birds! where must ye fly,
Now your water-pots are dry?
If ye stay upon the heath,
Ye'll be choak'd and clamm'd to death:
Therefore leave the shadeless goss,
 Seek the spring-head lin'd with moss;
There your little feet may stand,
Safely printing on the sand;
While, in full possession, where
Purling eddies ripple clear,
You with ease and plenty blest,
Sip the coolest and the best.
Then away! and wet your throats;
Cheer me with your warbling notes;
'Twill hot noon the more revive;
While I wander to contrive
For myself a place as good,
In the middle of a wood:
There aside some mossy bank,
Where the grass in bunches rank
Lifts its down on spindles high,
Shall be where I'll choose to lie;
Fearless of the things that creep,
There I'll think, and there I'll sleep;
Caring not to stir at all,
Till the dew begins to fall.

THE VILLAGE FUNERAL

To yon low church, with solemn-sounding knell,
  Which t'other day, as rigid fate decreed,
Mournfully knoll'd a Widow's passing-bell,
  The Village Funeral's warned to proceed.

Mournful indeed! the Orphans' friends are fled:
  Their Father's tender care has long been past;
The Widow's toil was all their hope of bread,
  And now the grave awaits to seize the last.

But that providing Power, for ever nigh,
  The universal friend of all distress,
Is sure to hear their supplicating cry,
  And prove a Father to the fatherless.

Now from the low mud cottage on the moor,
  By two and two sad bend the weeping train;
The coffin, ready near the propt-up door,
  Now slow proceeds along the wayward lane:

While, as they nearer draw in solemn state,
  The village neighbours are assembled round;
And seem with fond anxiety to wait
  The sad procession in the burial ground.

Yet every face the face of sorrow wears;
  And, now the solemn scene approaches nigh,
Each to make way for the slow march prepares,
  And on the coffin casts a serious eye.

Now walks the curate through the silent crowd,
  In snowy surplice loosely banded round;
Now meets the corse; and now he reads aloud,
  In mournful tone, along the burial ground.

The church they enter, and adown the aisle,
  Which more than usual wears a solemn hue,

They rest the coffin on set forms awhile,
Till the good priest performs the office due.

And though by duty aw'd to silence here,
The Orphans' griefs so piercing force a way;
And, oh! so moving do their griefs appear,
The worthy pastor kneels, in tears, to pray.

The funeral rites perform'd, by custom thought
A tribute sacred and essential here,
Now to the last, last place the body's brought,
Where all, dread fate! are summon'd to appear.

The church-yard round a mournful view displays,
Views where Mortality is plainly penn'd;
Drear seem the objects which the eye surveys,
As objects pointing to our latter end.

There the lank nettles sicken ere they seed,
Where from old trees eve's cordial vainly falls
To raise or comfort each dejected weed,
While pattering drops decay the crumbling walls.

Here stand, far distant from the pomp of Pride,
Mean little stones, thin scatter'd here and there;
By the scant means of Poverty applied,
The fond memorial of her friends to bear.

O Memory! thou sweet, enliv'ning power,
Thou shadow of that fame all hope to find;
The meanest soul exerts her utmost power
To leave some fragment of a name behind.

Now crowd the sad spectators round to see
The deep sunk grave, whose heap of swelling mold,
Full of the fragments of mortality,
Makes the heart shudder while the eyes behold.

Aw'd is the mind, by dreaded truths imprest,

To think that dust, which they before them see,
Once liv'd like them! Chill Conscience tells the rest:
That like that dust themselves must shortly be.

The gaping grave now claims its destin'd prey,
    "Ashes to ashes—dust to dust," is given;
The parent Earth receives her kindred clay,
    And the Soul starts to meet its home in heaven.

Ah, helpless Babes! now Grief in horror shrieks,
    Now Sorrow pauses dumb: each looker-on
Knows not the urging language which it speaks,—
    A friend—provider—this world's all—is gone!

Envy and Malice now have lost their aim,
    Slander's reproachful tongue can rail no more;
Her foes now pity, where they us'd to blame;
    The faults and foibles of this life are o'er.

The Orphans' grief and sorrow, so severe,
    To every heart in pity's language speak;
E'en the rough sexton can't withhold the tear,
    That steals unnotic'd down his furrow'd cheek.

Who but is griev'd to see the Fatherless
    Stroll with their rags unnotic'd through the street?
What eye but moistens at their sad distress,
    And sheds compassion's tear whene'er they meet?

Yon Workhouse stands as their asylum now,
    The place where Poverty demands to live;
Where parish Bounty scowls his scornful brow,
    And grudges the scant fare he's forc'd to give.

Oh, may I die before I'm doom'd to seek
    That last resource of hope, but ill supplied;
To claim the humble pittance once a week,
    Which justice forces from disdainful pride!—

Where the lost Orphan, lowly bending, weeps,
  Unnotic'd by the heedless as they pass,
There the grave closes where a Mother sleeps,
  With brambles platted on the tufted grass.

EARLY RISING

JUST at the early peep of dawn,
While brushing through the dewy lawn,
And viewing all the sweets of morn
                That shine at early rising;

Ere the ploughman yok'd his team,
Or sun had power to gild the stream,
Or woodlarks 'gan their morning hymn
                To hail its early rising;

With modest look and bashful eye,
Artless, innocent, and shy,
A lovely maiden pass'd me by,
                And charm'd my early rising.

Her looks had every power to wound,
Her voice had music in the sound,
When modestly she turn'd around
                To greet my early rising.

Good nature forc'd the maid to speak;
And good behaviour, not to seek,
Gave sweetness to her rosy cheek,
                Improv'd by early rising.

While brambles caught her passing by,
And her fine leg engag'd my eye,
Oh, who could paint confusion's dye,
                The blush of early rising!

While offering help to climb the stile,

A modest look and winning smile
(Love beaming in her eyes the while)
                    Repaid my early rising.

Aside the green hill's steepy brow,
Where shades the oak its darksome bough,
The maiden sat to milk her cow,
                    The cause of early rising.

The wild rose, mingling with the shade,
Stung with envy, clos'd to fade,
To see the rose her cheeks display'd,
                    The fruits of early rising.

The kiss desir'd—against her will,
To take the milk-pail up the hill,—
Seem'd from resistance sweeter still:
                    Thrice happy early rising!

And often since, aside the grove,
I've hied to meet the maid I love;
Repeating truths that time shall prove,
                    Which past at early rising.

May it be mine to spend my days
With her, whose beauty claims my praise;
Then joy shall crown my rural lays,
                    And bless my early rising.

TO A ROSE-BUD IN HUMBLE LIFE

SWEET, uncultivated blossom,
  Rear'd in spring's refreshing dews,
Dear to every gazer's bosom,
  Fair to every eye that views;
Opening bud, whose youth can charm us,
  Thine be many a happy hour;
Spreading rose, whose beauties warm us,

Flourish long, my lovely flower!

Though pride looks disdainful on thee,
  Scorning scenes so mean as thine,
Although fortune frowns upon thee,
  Lovely blossom, ne'er repine;
Health unbought is ever wi' thee,
  What their wealth can never gain;
Innocence doth garments gi'e thee,
  Such as fashion apes in vain.

When fit time and reason grant thee
  Leave to quit thy parent tree,
May some happy hand transplant thee
  To a station suiting thee:
On some lover's worthy bosom,
  May'st thou then thy sweets resign;
And may each unfolding blossom
  Open charms as sweet as thine.

Till that time, may joys unceasing
  Thy bard's every wish fulfil;
When that's come, may joys increasing
  Make thee blest and happier still:
Flourish fair, thou flower of Jessys;
  Pride of each admiring swain;
Envy of despairing lasses;
  Queen of Walkherd's lonely plain.

THE UNIVERSAL EPITAPH

No flattering praises daub my stone,
  My frailties and my faults to hide;
My faults and failings all are known—
  I liv'd in sin—in sin I died.

And oh! condemn me not, I pray,
  You who my sad confession view;

But ask your soul, if it can say,
That I'm a viler man than you.

FAMILIAR EPISTLE, TO A FRIEND

"Friendship, peculiar boon of heav'n,
The noblest mind's delight and pride;
To men and angels only giv'n,
To all the lower world denied:
Thy gentle flows of guiltless joys
On fools and villains ne'er descend,
In vain for thee the tyrant sighs,
And hugs a flatterer for a friend."
                                        JOHNSON.

THIS morning, just as I awoken,
A black cloud hung the south unbroken;
Thinks I, just now we'll have it soakin':
        I rightly guess'd.
'Faith! glad were I to see the token;
        I wanted rest.

And, 'fex! a pepp'ring day there's been on't;
But caution'd right with what I'd seen on't,
Keeping at home has kept me clean on't;
        Ye know my creed:
Fool-hardy work, I ne'er was keen on't—
        But let's proceed.

I write to keep from mischief merely,
Fire-side comforts 'joying cheerly;
And, brother chip, I love ye dearly,
        Poor as ye be!
With honest heart and soul, sincerely;
        They're all to me.

This scrawl, mark thou the application,
Though hardly worth thy observation,
Meaneth an humble invitation

On some day's end:
Of all ragg'd-muffins in the nation,
        Thou art the friend.

I've long been aggravated shocking,
To see our gentry folks so cocking:
But sorrow's often catch'd by mocking,
        The truth I've seen;
Their pride may want a shoe or stocking,
        For like has been.

Pride's power's not worth a roasted onion:
I'd's lief be prison mouse wi' Bunyan,
As I'd be king of our dominion,
        Or any other,
When shuffled through;—it's my opinion,
        One's good as t'other.

Nor would I gi'e, from off my cuff,
A single pin for all such stuff:
Riches—rubbish! a pinch of snuff
        Would dearly buy ye;
Who's got ye, keeps ye, that's enough:
        I don't envy ye.

If fate's so kind to let's be doing,
That's—just keep cart on wheels a going;
O'er my half-pint I can be crowing
        As well's another:
But when there's this and that stands owing,
        O curse the bother!

For had I money, like a many,
I'd balance, even to a penny.
Want! thy confinement makes me scranny:
        That spirit's mine,
I'd sooner gi'e than take from any;
        But Worth can't shine.

O Independence! oft I bait ye;
How blest I'd be to call ye matey!
Ye fawning, flattering slaves I hate ye:
        Mad, harum-scarum!
If rags and tatters under-rate me,
        Free still I'll wear 'em.

But hang all sorrows, now I'll bilk 'em;
What's past may go so: time that shall come,
As bad, or worse, or how it will come,
        I'll ne'er despair;
Poor as I am, friends shall be welcome
        As rich men's are.

So from my heart, old friend, I'll greet ye:
No outside brags shall ever cheat ye;
Wi' what I have, wi' such I'll treat ye,
        Ye may believe me;
I'll shake your rags whene'er I meet ye,
        If ye deceive me.

So mind ye, friend, what's what, I send it:
My letter's plain, and plain I'll end it:
Bad's bad enough, but worse won't mend it;
        So I'll be happy,
And while I've sixpence left I'll spend it
        In cheering nappy.

A hearty health shall crown my story:—
Dear, native England! I adore ye;
Britons, may ye with friends before ye
        Ne'er want a quart,
To drink your king and country's glory
        Wi' upright heart!

POSTSCRIPT

I've oft meant tramping o'er to see ye;
But, d—d old Fortune, (God forgi'e me!)
She's so cross-grain'd and forked wi' me,
    Be e'er so willing,
With all my jingling powers 'tint i' me
    To scheme a shilling.

And Poverty, with cursed rigour,
Spite of industry's utmost vigour,
Dizens me out in such a figure
    I'm 'sham'd being seen;
'Sides my old shoon, (poor Muse, ye twig her,)
    Wait roads being clean.

Then here wind-bound till Fate's conferr'd on't,
I wait ye, friend; and take my word on't,
I'll, spite of fate, scheme such a hoard on't,
    As we won't lack:
So no excuses shall be heard on't.
    Yours, random Jack.

THE HARVEST MORNING

COCKS wake the early morn with many a crow;
Loud striking village clock has counted four;
The labouring rustic hears his restless foe,
And weary, of his pains complaining sore,
Hobbles to fetch his horses from the moor:
Some busy 'gin to teem the loaded corn,
Which night throng'd round the barn's becrowded door;
Such plenteous scenes the farmer's yard adorn,
Such noisy, busy toils now mark the Harvest Morn.
The bird-boy's pealing horn is loudly blow'd;
The waggons jostle on with rattling sound;
And hogs and geese now throng the dusty road,
Grunting, and gabbling, in contention, round

The barley ears that litter on the ground.
What printing traces mark the waggon's way;
What busy bustling wakens echo round;
How drive the sun's warm beams the mist away;
How labour sweats and toils, and dreads the sultry day!

His scythe the mower o'er his shoulder leans,
And whetting, jars with sharp and tinkling sound,
Then sweeps again 'mong corn and crackling beans,
And swath by swath flops lengthening o"er the ground;
While 'neath some friendly heap, snug shelter'd round
From spoiling sun, lies hid the heart's delight;
And hearty soaks oft hand the bottle round,
Their toils pursuing with redoubled might—
Great praise to him be due that brought its birth to light.

Upon the waggon now, with eager bound,
The lusty picker whirls the rustling sheaves;
Or, resting ponderous creaking fork aground,
Boastful at once whole shocks of barley heaves:
The loading boy revengeful inly grieves
To find his unmatch'd strength and power decay;
The barley horn his garments interweaves;
Smarting and sweating 'neath the sultry day,
With muttering curses stung, he mauls the heaps away.

A motley group the clearing field surround:
Sons of Humanity, oh ne'er deny
The humble gleaner entrance in your ground;
Winter's sad cold, and Poverty are nigh.
Grudge not from Providence the scant supply:
You'll never miss it from your ample store.
Who gives denial,—harden'd, hungry hound,—
May never blessings crowd his hated door!
But he shall never lack, that giveth to the poor.

Ah, lovely Emma! mingling with the rest,
Thy beauties blooming in low life unseen,
Thy rosy cheeks, thy sweetly swelling breast;

But ill it suits thee in the stubs to glean.
O Poverty! how basely you demean
The imprison'd worth your rigid fates confine;
Not fancied charms of an Arcadian queen,
So sweet as Emma's real beauties shine:
Had Fortune blest, sweet girl, this lot had ne'er been thine.

The sun's increasing heat now mounted high,
Refreshment must recruit exhausted power;
The waggon stops, the busy tool's thrown by,
And 'neath a shock's enjoy'd the bevering hour.
The bashful maid, sweet health's engaging flower,
Lingering behind, o'er rake still blushing bends;
And when to take the horn fond swains implore,
With feign'd excuses its dislike pretends.
So pass the bevering-hours, so Harvest Morning ends.

O Rural Life! what charms thy meanness hide;
What sweet descriptions bards disdain to sing;
What loves, what graces on thy plains abide:
Oh, could I soar me on the Muse's wing,
What rifled charms should my researches bring!
Pleas'd would I wander where these charms reside;
Of rural sports and beauties would I sing;
Those beauties, Wealth, which you in vain deride,
Beauties of richest bloom, superior to your pride.

ON BEAUTY

BEAUTY, how changing and how frail!
   As skies in April showers,
Or as the summer's minute-gales,
   Or as the morning flowers.

As April skies, so beauty shades;
   As summer gales, so beauty flies;
As morning flower at evening fades,
   So beauty's tender blossom dies.

ON AN INFANT'S GRAVE

BENEATH the sod where smiling creep
  The daisies into view,
The ashes of an Infant sleep,
  Whose soul's as smiling too;
Ah! doubly happy, doubly blest,
  (Had I so happy been!)
Recall'd to heaven's eternal rest,
  Ere it knew how to sin.

Thrice happy Infant! great the bliss
  Alone reserv'd for thee;
Such joy 'twas my sad fate to miss,
  And thy good luck to see;

For oh! when all must rise again,
  And sentence then shall have,
What crowds will wish with me, in vain,
  They'd fill'd an infant's grave.

ON CRUELTY

COMPASSION sighs, and feels, and weeps,
  Retracing every pain
Inhuman man, in vengeance, heaps
  On all the lower train.

Ah, Pity! oft thy heart has bled,
  As galling now it bleeds;
And tender tears thy eyes have shed
  To witness cruel deeds.

The lash that weal'd poor Dobbin's hide,
  The strokes that cracking fall
On dogs, dumb cringing by thy side—
  Ah! thou hast felt them all.

The burthen'd asses, 'mid the laugh
  To see them whipp'd, would move
Thy soul to breathe in their behalf
  Humanity and love.

E'en 'plaining flies to thee have spoke,
  Poor trifles as they be;
And oft the spider's web thou'st broke,
  To set the captive me.

The pilfering mouse, entrapp'd and cag'd
  Within the wiry grate,
Thy pleading powers has oft engag'd
  To mourn its rigid fate.

How beat thy breast with conscious woes,
  To see the sparrows die:
Poor little thieves of many foes,
  Their food they dearly buy.

Where nature groans, where nature cries
  Beneath the butcher's knife,
How vain, how many were thy sighs,
  To save such guiltless life.

And ah! that most inhuman plan,
  Where reason's name's ador'd,
Unfriendly treatment—man to man—
  Thy tears have oft deplor'd.

Nor wise, nor good shall e'er deride
  The tear in Pity's eye;
Though laugh'd to scorn by senseless pride,
  From them it meets a sigh.

ON THE DEATH OF A BEAUTIFUL YOUNG LADY

YE meaner beauties cease your pride,
  Where borrow'd charms adorn;
Here nature aid of art defied,
  And blossom'd all its own.

The rose your paint but idly feigns,
  Bloom'd nature's brightest dyes;
The gems your wealthy pride sustains,
  Were natives of her eyes.

But what avails superior charms
  To boast of when in power,
Since, subject to a thousand harms,
  They perish like a flower.

Alas! we've nought to boast of here,
  And less to make us proud;
The brightest sun but rises clear
  To set behind a cloud.

Those charms which every heart subdue,
  Must all their powers resign;
Those eyes, like suns, too bright to view,
  Have now forgot to shine.

Her beauties so untimely fell,
  What mortal would be proud?
The day return'd, and found her well,
  But left her in her shroud.

To day the blossom buds and blooms,
  But who a day can trust?
Since the to-morrow, when it comes,
  Condemns it to the dust.

FALLING LEAVES

HAIL, falling Leaves! that patter round,
  Admonishers and friends;
Reflection wakens at the sound—
  So, Life, thy pleasure ends.

How frail the bloom, how short the stay,
  That terminates us all!
To day we flourish green and gay,
  Like leaves to-morrow fall.

Alas! how short is fourscore years,
  Life's utmost stretch,—a span;
And shorter still, when past, appears
  The vain, vain life of man.

These falling leaves once flaunted high,
  O pride! how vain to trust:
Now wither'd on the ground they lie,
  And mingled with the dust.

So Death serves all—and wealth and pride
  Must all their pomp resign;
E'en kings shall lay their crowns aside,
  To mix their dust with mine.

The leaves, how once they cloth'd the trees,
  None's left behind to tell;
The branch is naked to the breeze;
  We know not whence they fell.

A few more years, and I the same
  As they are now, shall be,
With nothing left to tell my name,
  Or answer, "Who was he?"

Green turf's allow'd forgotten heap
  Is all that I shall have,

Save that the little daisies creep
   To deck my humble grave.

THE CONTRAST OF BEAUTY AND VIRTUE

"Beauty's a transitory joy,
   "But Virtue's sweets shall never cloy."

AS o'er the gay pasture went rocking a clown,
A gay, gaudy Butter-cup's gold fringed gown
   Engag'd his attention, as passing her by;
And rudely to gain her he stooped adown,
   Its beauty so dazzled his eye.
By outside appearance the senseless are caught,
But Beauty's gay triumph is foolish and short;
   With nothing to gain the attention beside,
Possession soon sickens—and fleet as a thought,
   Beauty slips us forgotten aside.
As snifting and snufting the clodhopper goes,
And finding no sweetness for charming his nose,
   Frail Beauty's delusion soon wearied his eye;
And away the gay flowret he heedlessly throws,
   To wither unnotic'd, and die.

Ye young, giddy Wenches! gay Butter-cups! mind,
So tempting your dresses, your nature so kind,
   Virgin beauty once tasted, no longer endures;
The charm that should please us, fair Virtue, resign'd,
   A Butter-cup's fortune is yours.
Let Modesty's sweetness your blossoms adorn,
Be Virtue your guard, as the rose has her thorn;
   Then as chemists the sweets of the roses secure,—
When Beauty's no more, still to please is your own,
   For Virtue's charms ever endure.

TO AN APRIL DAISY

WELCOME, old Comrade! peeping once again;
 Our meeting 'minds me of a pleasant hour:
Spring's pencil pinks thee in that blushy stain,
 And Summer glistens in thy tinty flower.

Hail, Beauty's Gem! disdaining time nor place;
 Carelessly creeping on the dunghill's side;
Demeanour's softness in thy crimpled face
 Decks thee in beauties unattain'd by pride.

Hail, 'Venturer! once again that fearless here
 Encampeth on the hoar hill's sunny side;
Spring's early messenger! thou'rt doubly dear;
 And winter's frost by thee is well supplied.

Now winter's frowns shall cease their pelting rage,
 But winter's woes I need not tell to thee;
Far better luck thy visits well presage,
 And be it thine and mine that luck to see.

Ah, may thy smiles confirm the hopes they tell;
 To see thee frost-bit I'd be griev'd at heart;
I meet thee happy, and I wish thee well,
 Till ripening summer summons us to part.

Then like old mates, or two who've neighbours been,
 We'll part, in hopes to meet another year;
And o'er thy exit from this changing scene,
 We'll mix our wishes in a tokening tear.

TO HOPE

COME, flattering Hope! now woes distress me,
 Thy flattery I desire again;
Again rely on thee to bless me,
 To find thy vainness doubly vain.

Though disappointments vex and fetter,
    And jeering whisper thou art vain;
Still must I rest on thee for better,
    Still hope—and be deceiv'd again.

I can't but listen to thy prattle;
    I still must hug thee to my breast:
Like weaning child that's lost its rattle,
    Without my toy I cannot rest.

AN EFFUSION TO POESY, ON RECEIVING A DAMP FROM A GENTEEL OPINIONIST IN POETRY, OF SOME SWAY, AS I AM TOLD, IN THE LITERARY WORLD

DESPIS'D, unskill'd, or how I will,
Sweet Poesy! I'll love thee still;
Vain (cheering comfort!) though I be,
I still must love thee, Poesy.
A poor, rude clown, and what of that?
I cannot help the will of fate,
A lowly clown although I be;
Nor can I help it loving thee.
Still must I love thee, sweetest charm!
Still must my soul in raptures warm;
Still must my rudeness pluck the flower,
That's plucked in an evil hour,
While Learning scowls her scornful brow,
And damps my soul—I know not how.
Labour! 'cause thou'rt mean and poor,
Learning spurns thee from her door;
But despise me as she will,
Poesy! I love thee still.
When on pillow'd thorns I weep,
And vainly stretch me down to sleep;
Then, thou charm from heav'n above,
Comfort's cordial dost thou prove:
Then, engaging Poesy!
Then how sweet to talk with thee.

And be despis'd, or how I will,
I cannot help but love thee still.
Endearing charm! vain though I be,
I still must love thee, Poesy.
Still must I! ay, I can't refrain:
Damp'd, despis'd, or scorn'd again,
With vain, unhallow'd liberty
Still must I sing thee, Poesy.
And poor, and vain, and press'd beneath
Oppression's scorn although I be,
Still will I bind my simple wreath,
Still will I love thee, Poesy.

THE POET'S WISH

A WISH will rise in every breast,
For something more than what's possess'd;
Some trifle still, or more or less,
To make complete one's happiness.
And, faith! a wish will oft incline
To harbour in this breast of mine;
And oft old Fortune hears my case,
Told plain as nose upon her face;
But vainly do we beggars plead,
Although not ask'd before we need:
Old Fortune, like sly Farmer Dapple,
Where there's an orchard flings her apple;
But where there's no return to make ye,
She turns her nose up, "Deuce may take ye."
So rich men get their wealth at will,
And beggars—why, they're beggars still.

But 'tis not thought of being rich
That makes my wishing spirit itch;
'Tis just an independent fate,
Betwixt the little and the great;
No out-o'-the-way nor random wish;
No ladle crav'd for silver dish:
'Tis but a comfortable seat,

While without work both ends would meet.
'Tis just get hand to mouth with ease,
And read, and study as I please:
A little garret, warm and high,
 As loves the Muse sublime to fly,
With all my friends encircled round
In golden letters, richly bound;
Dear English poets! luckless fellows,
As born to such, so fate will tell us;
Might I their flow'ry themes peruse,
And be as happy in my Muse,
Like them sublimely high to soar,
Without their fate—so cursed poor!
While one snug room, not over small,
Contain'd my necessary all;
And night and day left me secure
'Mong books, my chiefest furniture;
With littering papers, many a bit
Scrawl'd by the Muse in fancied fit.
And curse upon that routing jade,
My territories to invade,
Who finds me out in evil hour,
To brush, and clean, and scrub, and scour;
And with a dreaded brush or broom
 Disturbs my learned lumber-room.
Such busy things I hate to see,
Such troublers ne'er shall trouble me:
Let dust keep gathering on the ground,
And roping cobwebs dangle round;
Let spiders weave their webs at will;
Would cash, when wanted, pockets fill,
To *pint* it just at my desire,
My drooping Muse with ale inspire,
And fetch at least a roll of bread,
Without a debt to run or dread.
Such comforts, would they were but mine,
To something more I'd ne'er incline:
But happiest then of happy clowns,
 I'd sing all cares away;

And pitying monarchs capp'd with crowns,
  I'd see more joys than they.

  Thus wish'd a bard, whom fortune scorns,
To find a rose among the thorns;
And musing o'er each heavy care,
His pen stuck useless in his hair,
His muse was dampt, nor fir'd his soul,
And still unearn'd his penny roll;
Th' unfinish'd labours of his head
Were listless on the table spread;
When lo! to bid him hope no more,
A rap—an earthquake! jars the door;
His heart drops in his shoes with doubt:
"What fiend has found my lodging out?"
Poor trembling tenants of the quill!—
"Here, sir, I bring my master's bill."—
He heav'd a sigh, and scratch'd his head,
And credit's mouth with promise fed:
Then sat in terror down again,
Invok'd the Muse, and scrigg'd a strain;
A trifling something glad to get,
To earn a dinner; and discharge the debt.

SUMMER EVENING

THE sinking sun is taking leave,
And sweetly gilds the edge of Eve,
While huddling clouds of purple dye,
Gloomy hang the western sky.
Crows crowd croaking over head,
Hastening to the woods to bed.
Cooing sits the lonely dove,
Calling home her absent love.
With "Kirchup! kirchup!" 'mong the wheats,
Partridge distant partridge greets;
Beckoning hints to those that roam,
That guide the squander'd covey home.
Swallows check their winding flight,

And twittering on the chimney light.
Round the pond the martins flirt,
Their snowy breasts bedaub'd with dirt,
While the mason, 'neath the slates,
Each mortar-bearing bird awaits:
By art untaught, each labouring spouse
Curious daubs his hanging house.
Bats flit by in hood and cowl;
Through the barn-hole pops the owl;
From the hedge, in drowsy hum,
Heedless buzzing beetles bum,
Haunting every bushy place,
Flopping in the labourer's face.
Now the snail hath made his ring;
And the moth with snowy wing
Circles round in winding whirls,
Through sweet evening's sprinkled pearls,
On each nodding rush besprent;
Dancing on from bent to bent:
Now to downy grasses clung,
Resting for a while he's hung;
Then, to ferry o'er the stream,
Vanishing as flies a dream;
Playful still his hours to keep,
Till his time has come to sleep;
In tall grass, by fountain head,
Weary then he drops to bed.
From the hay-cock's moisten'd heaps,
Startled frogs take vaunting leaps;
And along the shaven mead,
Jumping travellers, they proceed:
Quick the dewy grass divides,
Moistening sweet their speckled sides;
From the grass or flowret's cup,
Quick the dew-drop bounces up.
Now the blue fog creeps along,
And the bird's forgot his song:
Flowers now sleep within their hoods;
Daisies button into buds;

From soiling dew the butter-cup
Shuts his golden jewels up;
Wait again the smiles of day.
'Neath the willow's wavy boughs,
Dolly, singing, milks her cows;
While the brook, as bubbling by,
Joins in murmuring melody.
Dick and Dob, with jostling joll,
Homeward drag the rumbling roll;
Whilom Ralph, for Doll to wait,
Lolls him o'er the pasture gate.
Swains to fold their sheep begin;
Dogs loud barking drive them in.
Hedgers now along the road
Homeward bend beneath their load;
And from the long furrow'd seams,
Ploughmen loose their weary teams:
Ball, with urging lashes weal'd,
Still so slow to drive a-field,
Eager blundering from the plough,
Wants no whip to drive him now;
At the stable-door he stands,
Looking round for friendly hands
To loose the door its fast'ning pin,
And let him with his corn begin.
Round the yard, a thousand ways,
Beasts in expectation gaze,
Catching at the loads of hay
Passing fodd'rers tug away.
Hogs with grumbling, deaf'ning noise,
Bother round the server boys;
And, far and near, the motley group
Anxious claim their suppering-up.
From the rest, a blest release,
Gabbling home, the quarreling geese
Seek their warm straw-litter'd shed,
And, waddling, prate away to bed.
'Nighted by unseen delay,
Poking hens, that lose their way,

On the hovel's rafters rise,
Slumbering there, the fox's prize.
Now the cat has ta'en her seat,
With her tail curl'd round her feet;
Patiently she sits to watch
Sparrows fighting on the thatch.
Now Doll brings th' expected pails,
And dogs begin to wag their tails;
With strokes and pats they're welcom'd in,
And they with looking wants begin:
Slove in the milk-pail brimming o'er,
She pops their dish behind the door.
Prone to mischief boys are met,
'Neath the eaves the ladder's set,
Sly they climb in softest tread,
To catch the sparrow on his bed;
Massacred, O cruel pride!
Dash'd against the ladder's side.
Curst barbarians! pass me by;
Come not, Turks, my cottage nigh;
Sure my sparrows are my own,
Let ye then my birds alone.
Come, poor birds! from foes severe
Fearless come, you're welcome here;
My heart yearns at fate like yours,
A sparrow's life's as sweet as ours.
Hardy clowns! grudge not the wheat
Which hunger forces birds to eat:
Your blinded eyes, worst foes to you,
Can't see the good which sparrows do.
Did not poor birds with watching rounds
Pick up the insects from your grounds,
Did they not tend your rising grain,
You then might sow to reap in vain.
Thus Providence, right understood,
Whose end and aim is doing good,
Sends nothing here without its use;
Though ignorance loads it with abuse,
And fools despise the blessing sent,

And mock the Giver's good intent.—
O God! let me what's good pursue,
Let me the same to others do
As I'd have others do to me,
And learn at least humanity.

Dark and darker glooms the sky;
Sleep 'gins close the labourer's eye:
Dobson leaves his greensward seat,
Neighbours where they neighbours meet
Crops to praise, and work in hand,
And battles tell from foreign land.
While his pipe is puffing out,
Sue he's putting to the rout,
Gossiping, who takes delight
To shool her knitting out at night,
And back-bite neighbours 'bout the town—
Who's got new caps, and who a gown,
And many a thing, her evil eye
Can see they don't come honest by.
Chattering at a neighbour's house,
She hears call out her frowning spouse;
Prepar'd to start, she soodles home,
Her knitting twirling o'er her thumb,
As, loth to leave, afraid to stay,
She bawls her story all the way:
The tale so fraught with 'ticing charms,
Her apron folded o'er her arms,
She leaves the unfinished tale, in pain,
To end as evening comes again;
And in the cottage gangs with dread,
To meet old Dobson's timely frown,
Who grumbling sits, prepar'd for bed,
While she stands chelping 'bout the town.

The night-wind now, with sooty wings,
In the cotter's chimney sings:
Now, as stretching o'er the bed,
Soft I raise my drowsy head,

Listening to the ushering charms
That shake the elm tree's mossy arms;
Till sweet slumbers stronger creep,
  Deeper darkness stealing round,
Then, as rock'd, I sink to sleep,
  'Mid the wild wind's lulling sound.

SUMMER MORNING

THE cocks have now the morn foretold,
  The sun again begins to peep;
The shepherd, whistling to his fold,
  Unpens and frees the captive sheep.

O'er pathless plains, at early hours,
  The sleepy rustic sloomy goes;
The dews, brush'd off from grass and flowers,
  Bemoistening sop his harden'd shoes;

For every leaf that forms a shade,
  And every flowret's silken top,
And every shivering bent and blade,
  Stoops, bowing with a diamond drop.

But soon shall fly those pearly drops,
  The red, round sun advances higher;
And stretching o'er the mountain tops,
  Is gilding sweet the village spire.

Again the bustling maiden seeks
  Her cleanly pail, and eager now,
Rivals the morn with rosy cheeks,
  And hastens off to milk her cow;

While echo tells of Colin near,
  Blithe, whistling o'er the misty hills:
The powerful magic fills her ear,
  And through her beating bosom thrills.

'Tis sweet to meet the morning breeze,
　Or list the giggling of the brook;
Or, stretch'd beneath the shade of trees,
　Peruse and pause on Nature's book;

When Nature every sweet prepares
　To entertain our wish'd delay,—
The images which morning wears,
　The wakening charms of early day!

Now let me tread the meadow paths,
　While glittering dew the ground illumes,
As, sprinkled o'er the withering swaths,
　Their moisture shrinks in sweet perfumes;

And hear the beetle sound his horn;
　And hear the skylark whistling nigh,
Sprung from his bed of tufted corn,
　A hailing minstrel in the sky.

First sunbeam, calling Night away,
　To see how sweet thy summons seems,
Split by the willow's wavy grey,
　And sweetly dancing on the streams:

How fine the spider's web is spun,
　Unnoticed to vulgar eyes;
Its silk thread glittering in the sun
　Art's bungling vanity defies.

Roaming while the dewy fields
　'Neath their morning burthen lean,
While its crop my searches shields,
　Sweet I scent the blossom'd bean:

Making oft remarking stops;
　Watching tiny nameless things
Climb the grass's spiry tops,
　Ere they try their gauzy wings.

So emerging into light,
    From the ignorant and vain,
Fearful Genius takes her flight,
    Skimming o'er the lowly plain.

Now in gay, green, glossy coat,
    On the shivering, benty balk,
The free grasshopper chirps his note,
    Bounding on from stalk to stalk.

And the bee at early hours
    Sips the tawny bean's perfumes;
While butterflies infest the flowers,
    Just to shew their glossy plumes.

So Industry oft seeks the sweets,
    Which weary labour ought to gain;
And oft the bliss the idle meets,
    And heaven bestows the bliss in vain.

Pleas'd I list the rural themes
    Heartening up the ploughman's toil;
Urging on the jingling teams,
    As they turn the mellow soil.

Industry's care abounds again,
    As now the peace of night is gone;
Many a murmur wakes the plain,
    Many a waggon rumbles on.

The swallow wheels his circling flight,
    And o'er the water's surface skims;
Then on the cottage chimney lights,
    And twittering chants his morning hymns.

Station'd high, a towering height,
    On the sun-gilt weathercock,
Now the jackdaw takes his flight,
    Frighted by the striking clock.

Snug the wary watching thrush
  Sits to prune her speckled breast,
Where the woodbine, round the bush
  Weaving, hides her mortar'd nest,—

Till the cows, with hungry low,
  Pick the rank grass from her bower;
Startled then—dead leaves below
  Quick receive the pattering shower.

Now the scythe the morn salutes,
  In the meadow tinkling soon;
While on mellow-tootling flutes
  Sweetly breathes the shepherd's tune.

Where the bank the stream o'erlooks,
  And the wreathing worms are found,
Anglers sit to bait their hooks,
  On the hill with wild thyme crown'd.

While, the treach'rous watching stork
  With the heedless gudgeon flies,
Bobbing sinks the vanish'd cork,
  And the roach becomes a prize.

'Neath the black-thorn's stunted bush,
  Cropp'd by wanton oxen down,
Whistling o'er each culling rush,
  Cow-boys plat a rural crown.

As slow the hazy mists retire,
  Crampt circle's more distinctly seen;
Thin scatter'd huts, and neighbouring spire,
  Drop in to stretch the bounded scene.

Brisk winds the lighten'd branches shake,
  By pattering, plashing drops confess'd;
And, where oaks dripping shade the lake,
  Print crimpling dimples on its breast.

The misted brook, its edges reek;
   Sultry Noon is drawing on;
The east has lost its ruddy streak,
   And Morning sweets are almost gone.

Now as Morning takes her leave,
   And while swelter'd Nature mourns,
Let me, waiting soothing Eve,
   Seek my cot till she returns.

DAWNINGS OF GENIUS

GENIUS! a pleasing rapture of the mind,
A kindling warmth to learning unconfin'd,
Glows in each breast, flutters in every vein,
From art's refinement to th' uncultur'd swain.
Hence is that warmth the lowly shepherd proves,
Pacing his native fields and willow groves;
Hence is that joy, when every scene unfolds,
Which taste endears and latest memory holds;
Hence is that sympathy his heart attends,
When bush and tree companions seem and friends;
Hence is that fondness from his soul sincere,
That makes his native place so doubly dear.
In those low paths which Poverty surrounds,
The rough rude ploughman, off his fallow-grounds,
(That necessary tool of wealth and pride,)
While moil'd and sweating by some pasture's side,
Will often stoop inquisitive to trace
The opening beauties of a daisy's face;
Oft will he witness, with admiring eyes,
The brook's sweet dimples o'er the pebbles rise;
And often, bent as o'er some magic spell,
He'll pause, and pick his shaped stone and shell:
Raptures the while his inward powers inflame,
And joys delight him which he cannot name;
Ideas picture pleasing views to mind,
For which his language can no utterance find;
Increasing beauties, fresh'ning on his sight,

Unfold new charms, and witness more delight;
So while the present please, the past decay,
And in each other, losing, melt away.
Thus pausing wild on all he saunters by,
He feels enraptur'd though he knows not why;
And hums and mutters o'er his joys in vain,
And dwells on something which he can't explain.
The bursts of thought with which his soul's perplex'd,
Are bred one moment, and are gone the next;
Yet still the heart will kindling sparks retain,
And thoughts will rise, and Fancy strive again.
So have I mark'd the dying ember's light,
When on the hearth it fainted from my sight,
With glimmering glow oft redden up again,
And sparks crack brightening into life, in vain;
Still lingering out its kindling hope to rise,
Till faint, and fainting, the last twinkle dies.
   Dim burns the soul, and throbs the fluttering heart,
Its painful pleasing feelings to impart;
Till by successless sallies wearied quite,
The Memory fails, and Fancy takes her flight.
The wick confin'd within its socket dies,
Borne down and smother'd in a thousand sighs.

TO A COLD BEAUTY, INSENSIBLE OF LOVE

ELIZA, farewel! ah, most lovely Eliza,
   So much as thy beauties excel;
So much as I love thee, so much as I prize thee,
   Unfeeling Eliza, farewel!
The heart without feeling, the beauty's but small,
   Though tempting it be to the view;
The warmth of a soul crowns the beauty of all,
   Without it thou'rt nothing—Adieu!
Thou Image of Beauty, endeavour is vain
   To warm thee to life and to love,
Could I but the skill of the artist attain,
   And steal thee a soul from above;

Though as fair as the statue he finish'd art thou,
  'Twere folly his plan to pursue;
I would give thee feeling, but cannot tell how;
  I would love thee, dear—but, adieu!

To all that life sweetens eternally lost,
  Where love makes a heaven below,
Thy bosom's congealed in apathy's frost,
  As white and as cold as the snow:
Since no spark of soul its dead tenant can warm,
  Thou Icicle hung on Spring's brow,
I'll turn my sighs from thee to mix with the storm;
  The storm's full as tender as thou.

That heart where no feelings or raptures can dwell,
  Be its owner in person most fair,
Where beauty a bargain to buy or to sell,
  I never would purchase it there:
So cold to the joys that in sympathy burn
  Joys none but true love ever knew,
How lost should I be could I prove no return:
  I wish to be happy—Adieu!

PATTY

YE swampy falls of pasture ground,
  And rushy spreading greens;
Ye rising swells in brambles bound,
  And freedom's wilder'd scenes;
I've trod ye oft, and love ye dear,
  And kind was fate to let me;
On you I found my all, for here
  'Twas first my Patty met me.
Flow on, thou gently plashing stream,
  O'er weed-beds wild and rank;
Delighted I've enjoy'd my dream
  Upon thy mossy bank:
Bemoistening many a weedy stem,

I've watch'd thee wind so clearly;
And on thy bank I found the gem
That makes me love thee dearly.

Thou wilderness, so rudely gay;
Oft as I seek thy plain,
Oft as I wend my steps away,
And meet my joys again,
And brush the weaving branches by
Of briars and thorns so matty;
So oft Reflection warms a sigh,—
Here first I met my Patty.

ON YOUTH

AH, Youth's sweet joys! why are ye gone astray?
Fain would I follow could I find a plan:
To my great loss are ye exchang'd away
For that sad sorrow-ripening name—a Man.
Far distant joys! the prospect gives me pain:
Ah, Happiness! and hast thou no return?
No kind concern to call thee back again,
And bid this aching bosom cease to mourn?
The daisies' hopes have met another Spring,
Poor standard tenants on a stormy plain;
The lark confirms it on his russet wing;
And why alone am I denied?—In vain:
Ah, Youth is fled!
A second blossom I but vainly crave:
The flower, that opes with peace to come,
Is budding in the grave.

THE ADIEU

LONE Lodge in the bend of the valley, farewel!
Thou spot, ever dear to my view;
My anguish my bosom's forbidden to tell,
While wandering I bid thee adieu.
Stain'd Rose-bud! thou once of my ballad the pride,

Till proof brought thy canker to view;
Though heedlessly now thou hast roam'd from thy guide,
I still wish thy foes may be few.

My love thou hast never yet known to deceive,
I vow'd ever constant to be;
And thy faithful returns did as firmly believe,
Till proof found a failing in thee.
Thou'rt lovely, I own it in many a sigh,
But what has such beauty to win?
The night-shade, it blossoms as fair to the eye,
That harbours dead poison within.

O Rose-bud! thou subject of many a song,
Thy defilement's too plain to my view;
I love thee, but cannot forgive thee the wrong;
I hope, but it's vainly:—adieu!
Resolv'd never more to behold you again,
Or to visit the spot where you dwell,
My last look I'm leaving on Walkherd's lov'd plain,
My last vow I'm breathing—Farewel!

CRAZY NELL: A TRUE STORY

THE sun was low sinking behind the far trees,
And, crossing the path, humming home were the bees;
And darker and darker it grew by degrees,
    And crows they flock'd quawking to rest:
When, unknown to her parents, Nell slove on her hat,
And o'er the fields hurried—scarce knew she for what;
But her sweetheart, in taking advantage and that,
    Had kiss'd, and had promis'd the best.

Poor maidens! of husbands so much they conceit,
The daisy scarce touch'd rose unhurt from her feet,
So eager she hasten'd her lover to meet,
    As to make him to wait was unjust;
On the wood, dim discover'd, she fixed her eyes—

Such a queer spot to meet in—suspicions might rise;
But the fond word "a sweetheart" such goodness implies,
　　Ah, who would a lover distrust!

More gloomy and darker—black clouds hung the wind,
Far objects diminish'd before and behind,
More narrow and narrow the circle declin'd,
　　And silence reign'd awfully round,
When Nelly within the wood-riding sat down;
She listen'd, and lapp'd up her arms in her gown;
Far, far from her cottage, and far from the town,
And her sweetheart not yet to be found.

The minutes seem'd hours—with impatience she heard
The flap of a leaf, and the twit of a bird;
The least little trifle that whisper'd or stirr'd,
　　Hope pictur'd her lover as nigh:
When wearied with sitting, she wander'd about,
And open'd the wood-gate, and gave a look out;
And fain would have halloo'd, but Fear had a doubt
　　That thieves might be lurking hard by.

Far clocks count eleven—"He won't be long now,"
Her anxious hopes whisper'd—hoarse wav'd the wood bough;
—"He heeds not my fears, or he's false to his vow!"
　　Poor Nelly sat doubtful, and sigh'd:
The man who had promis'd her husband to be,
And to wed on the morrow—her friends all could see
That a good-for-nought sort of a fellow was he,
　　And they hoped nothing worse might betide.

At length, as in fear, slowly tapp'd the wood-gate;
'Twas Ben!—she complain'd so long painful to wait:
Deep design hung his looks, he but mumbled "'Tis late,"
　　And pass'd her, and bid her come on.
The mind plainly pictures that *night-hour* of dread,
In the midst of a wood! where the trees over head
The darkness increased—a dungeon they spread,
　　And the clock at the moment toll'd one!

Nell fain would have forc'd, as she follow'd, some chat;
And trifled, on purpose, with this thing and that;
And complain'd of the dew-droppings spoiling her hat;
    But nothing Ben's silence would break.
Extensive the forest, the roads to and fro,
And this way and that way, above and below,
As crossing the ridings, as winding they go—
    "Ah! what road or way can he seek?"

Her eye, ever watchful, now caught an alarm;
Lights gleam, and tools tinkle, as if nigh a farm:
"O don't walk so fast, Ben—I'm fearful of harm!"
    She said, and shrugg'd closer behind.
"That light's from my house!" 'twas the first word she caught
From his lips, since he through the dark wood had her brought.
A house in a wood! Oh, good God! what a thought;
    What sensations then rush'd on her mind!

The things, which her friends and her neighbours had said,
Afresh at that moment all jump'd in her head;
And mistrust, for the first time, now fill'd her with dread:
    And as she approach'd, she could see
How better, for her, their advice to have ta'en;
And she wish'd to herself then she had—but in vain:
—A heap of fresh mould, and a spade, she saw plain,
    And a lantern tied up to a tree.

 "Here they come!" a voice whispers;—"Haste! put out the
light."
"No: dig the grave deeper!"—"Very dark is the night."
Slow mutterings mingled.—Oh, dismal the sight!
    —The fate of poor Nelly was plain.
Fear chill'd through her heart—but Hope whisper'd her—Fly!
Chance seiz'd on the moment, a wind-gust blew high,
She slipt in the thicket—he turn'd not his eye,
    And the grave-diggers waited in vain.

At that fearful moment, so dreadfully dark,

How welcome the song of the shepherd, or lark;
How cheery to listen, and hear the dog bark,
   As through the dark wood she fled fast:
But, horror of horrors, all nature was hush!
Not a sound was there heard—save a blackbird, or thrush,
That, started from sleep, flusker'd out of the bush,
   Which her brushing clothes shook as they past.

Fear now truly pictur'd: she ne'er turn'd her head
Either this way or that way—straight forward she fled;
And Fancy, still hearing the horrors with dread,
   On faster and fearfuller stole.
The matted leaves rustle—the boughs swiftly part,
Her hands and her face with the brambles did smart;
But, oh! the worst anguish was felt at her heart,—
   Ben's unkindness struck death to her soul.

Now glimmering lighter the forest appears,
And Hope, the sweet comforter, soften'd her fears;
Light and liberty, Darkness! thy horror endears;
   Great bliss did the omen
impart:
The forest, its end, and its terrors gone by,
She breath'd the free air, and she saw the blue sky;
Her own fields she knew—to her home did she fly,
   And great was the joy of her heart.

Oh, prospect endearing! the village to view,
The morn sweet appearing,—and gay the cock crew,
When, mangled by brambles and dabbled in dew,
   She gave a loud rap at the door:
The parents in raptures wept over their child;
She mutter'd her terrors—her eyes rolled wild—
"They dig the grave deeper!—Your Nelly's beguil'd!"
   She said, and she siled on the floor.

Poor Nell soon recover'd; but, ah! to her cost,
Her sense and her reason for ever were lost:
And scorch'd by the summer, and chill'd by the frost,

A maniac, restless and wild,
Now crazy Nell rambles; and still she will weep,
And, fearless, at night into hovels will creep.—
Fond parents! alas, their affliction is deep,
   And vainly they comfort their child.

DOLLY'S MISTAKE; OR, THE WAYS OF THE WAKE

ERE the sun o'er the hills, round and red, 'gan a peeping,
   To beckon the chaps to their ploughs,
Too thinking and restless all night to be sleeping,
   I brush'd off to milking my cows;
To get my jobs forward, and eager preparing
   To be off in time to the wake,
Where yielding so freely a kiss for a fairing,
   I made a most shocking mistake.

Young Ralph met me early, and off we were steering,
   I cuddled me close to his side;
The neighbours, while passing, my fondness kept jeering,
   "Young Ralph's timely suited!" they cried.
But he bid me mind not their evil pretensions,
   "Fools mun," says he, "talk for talk's sake;"
And, kissing me, "Doll, if you've any 'prehensions,
   "Let me tell you, my wench, you mistake."

My cows when we pass'd them kept booing and mooing,
   In truth, but they made me to stare;
As much as to say, "Well, now, Dolly, you're going,
   Mind how you get on at the fair."
While bidden "good speed" from each gazing beholder,
   "Good journey away to the wake,"
The mowers stopp'd whetting, to look o'er their shoulder,
   Saying "Dolly, don't make a mistake."

I couldn't but mind the fine morning so charming,
   The dew-drops they glitter'd like glass;
And all o'er the meads were the buttercups swarming,
   Like so many suns in the grass;

I thought as we pass'd them, if such a thing could be,
    What a fine string of beads they would make;
But when I could think of such nonsense, it would be
    Because I had made no mistake.

So on his arm hanging, with stories beguiling,
    Of what he would buy me when there,
The road cutting short with his kissing and smiling,
    He 'veigl'd me off to the fair:
Such presents he proffer'd before I could claim 'em,
    To keep while I liv'd for his sake,
And what I lik'd best, o'er and o'er begg'd me name 'em,
    That he mightn't go make a mistake.

And, lud, what a crushing and crowding were wi' 'em,
    What noises are heard at a fair;
Here some sell so cheap, as they'd even go gi' 'em,
    If conscience would take, they declare:
Some so good, 'tis e'en worth more than money to buy 'em,
    Fine gingerbread nuts and plum-cake;
For truth they bid Ralph, ere he treated me, try 'em,
    And then there could be no mistake.

A sly Merry Andrew was making his speeches,
    With chaps and girls round him a
swarm,
And, "Mind," said he, fleering, "ye chubby-fac'd witches,
    Your fairings don't do you some harm."
The hay-cocks he nam'd, in the meads passing by 'em,
    When weary we came from the wake,
So soft, so inviting, for rest we mun try 'em;
    What a fool should I be to mistake.

But promis'd so faithful, behaviour so clever,
    Such gifts as Ralph cramm'd in my hand,
How could I distrust of his goodness? O never!
    And who could his goodness withstand?
His ribbons, his fairings, past counting, or nearly,
    Some return when he press'd me to make,

Good manners mun give, while he lov'd me so dearly:
  Ah! where could I see the mistake?

'Till dark night he kept me, with fussing and lying,
  How he'd see me safe home to my cot;
Poor maiden, so easy, so free in complying,
  I the showman's good caution forgot:
All bye-ways he led me, 'twas vain to dispute it,
  The moon blush'd for shame, naughty rake!
Behind a cloud sneaking—but darkness well suited
  His baseness, who caus'd the mistake.

In vain do I beg him to wed and have done wi't,
  So fair as he promis'd we should;
We cou'dn't do worse than as how we've begun wi't,
  Let matters turn out as they would:
But he's always a talking 'bout wedding expenses,
  And the wages he's gotten to take;
Too plain can I see through his evil pretences,
  Too late I find out the mistake.

Oh, what mun I do with my mother reprovin',
  Since she will do nothing but chide?
For when old transgressors have been in the oven,
  They know where the young ones may hide.
In vain I seek pity with plaints and despairings,
  Always ding'd on the nose with the wake:
Young maidens! be cautious who give you your fairings;
  You see what attends a mistake.

MY MARY

WHO lives where beggars rarely speed,
And leads a hum-drum life indeed,
As none beside herself would lead?
                    My Mary.

Who lives where noises never cease,
And what with hogs, and ducks, and geese,

Can never have a minute's peace?

> My Mary.

Who, nearly battled to her chin,
Bangs down the yard through thick and thin,
Nor picks her road, nor cares a pin?

> My Mary.

Who, save in Sunday's bib and tuck,
Goes daily waddling like a duck,
O'er head and ears in grease and muck?

> My Mary.

Unus'd to pattens or to clogs,
Who takes the swill to serve the hogs,
And steals the milk for cats and dogs?

> My Mary.

Who, frost and snow, as hard as nails,
Stands out o'doors, and never fails
To wash up things and scour the pails?

> My Mary.

Who bustles night and day, in short,
At all catch jobs of every sort,
And gains her mistress' favour for't?

> My Mary.

And who is oft repaid with praise,
In doing what her mistress says,
And yielding to her whimmy ways?

> My Mary.

For there's none apter, I believe,
At "creeping up a mistress' sleeve,"
Than this low kindred stump of Eve,

> My Mary.

Who, when the baby's all unfit,

To please its mamma kisses it,
And vows no rose on earth's so sweet?
                                My Mary.

But when her mistress is not nigh,
Who swears, and wishes it would die,
And pinches it and makes it cry?
                                My Mary.

Oh, rank deceit! what soul could think—
But gently there, revealing ink:
At faults of thine thy friend must wink,
                                My Mary.

Who, not without a "spark o'pride,"
Though strong as grunter's bristly hide,
Doth keep her hair in papers tied?
                                My Mary.

And, mimicking the gentry's way,
Who strives to speak as fine as they,
And minds but every word they say?
                                My Mary.

And who, though's well bid blind to see,
As her to tell ye A from B,
Thinks herself none o' low degree?
                                My Mary.

Who prates and runs o'er silly stuff,
And 'mong the boys makes sport enough,
So ugly, silly, droll and rough?
                                My Mary.

Ugly! Muse, for shame of thee,
What faults art thou a going to see
In one, that's 'lotted, out to be
                                My Mary?

Who, low in stature, thick and fat,
Turns brown from going without a hat,
Though not a pin the worse for that?
      My Mary.

Who's laugh'd at too by every whelp,
For failings which she cannot help?
But silly fools will laugh and chelp,
      My Mary.

For though in stature mighty small,
And near as thick as thou art tall,
The hand made thee, that made us all,
      My Mary.

And though thy nose hooks down too much,
And prophesies thy chin to touch;
I'm not so nice to look at such,
      My Mary.

No, no; about thy nose and chin,
Its hooking out, or bending in,
I never heed or care a pin,
      My Mary.

And though thy skin is brown and rough,
And form'd by nature hard and tough,
All suiteth me! so that's enough,
      My Mary.

SONGS AND BALLADS

UPON A PLAIN: A BALLAD

UPON the plain there liv'd a swain,
  A flock his whole employ;
Unknown love's cares, and all its snares,
  To damp his humble joy.

Industry toils, while Fortune smiles,
  To bless him with increase;
Contentment made his humble trade
  A scene of health and peace.

But Cupid sly, whose jealous eye
  Envied his happiness,
With pointed darts and subtle arts
  Resolv'd on his distress.

Though first in vain he work'd his brain,
  Yet, practis'd in deceit,
Fresh schemes and plans were nigh his hands;
  And some were sure to hit.

In fatal hour he prov'd his power;
  A shepherd's form he's ta'en,
With crook and song he hums along,
  And thus accosts the swain:

"Go, Friend," he cried, "to yonder side
  The hedge that bounds the plain,
For there a lamb has lost its dam,
  And bleats for help in vain."

Intent to start, his tender heart
  O'erlooks the subtle snare;
The swain's beguil'd, pleas'd Cupid smil'd,—
  Fair Florimel was there.

The roses red her cheeks bespread,
    Her bosom's lily white;
To view her charms each bosom warms,
    Enraptur'd at the sight.

Her heaving breast, her slender waist,
    Her shape genteel and tall,
Her charms divine unrivall'd shine,
    Alike confess'd by all.

Beneath the shade, the lovely maid
    Lay shelter'd from the sun.
O luckless swain! go, fly the plain,
    Or stay and be undone.

For, ah! 'twas prov'd, by them that lov'd,
    She own'd a scornful eye;
Her pride was vain, the way to gain
    Her pity, was to die.

Stretch'd on the green, her beauty's seen
    To all advantage there;
To meet the breeze that fann'd the trees,
    Her snowy neck was bare.

She meets his view; sweet Peace, adieu!
    And pleasures known before:
He sighs, approves, admires, and loves;
    His heart's his own no more.

FRIEND LUBIN

FRIEND Lubin loves his Saturdays,
    That bring him rest on Sundays;
But *Whittler* loves contrary ways,
    And wishes all were Mondays.
The Labourer doats on welcome night
    To rest his weary limbs;
And Misses in the day delight,

To shew their dressy whims.

But oh, the day and night to me,
  The Saturday or Monday,
I care not which-a-way they be,
  Or working day or Sunday

Oh no, I care not what they be,
  Though night I most approve;
But oh, the day is dear to me,
  That brings me to my love.

PATTY OF THE VALE

WHERE lonesome woodlands close surrounding
  Mark the spot a solitude,
And nature's uncheck'd scenes abounding
  Form a prospect wild and rude,
A cottage cheers the spot so glooming,
  Hid in the hollow of the dale,
Where, in youth and beauty blooming,
  Lives sweet Patty of the Vale.

Gay as the lambs her cot surrounding,
  Sporting wild the shades among,
O'er the hills and bushes bounding,
  Artless, innocent, and young,
Fresh, as blush of morning roses
  Ere the mid-day suns prevail,
Fair, as lily-bud uncloses,
  Blooms sweet Patty of the Vale.

Low and humble though her station,
  Dress though mean she's doom'd to wear,
Few superiors in the nation
  With her beauty can compare.
What are riches?—not worth naming,
  Though with some they may prevail;
Their's be choice of wealth proclaiming,

Mine is Patty of the Vale.

Fools may fancy wealth and fortune
　　Join to make a happy pair,
And for such the god importune,
　　With full many a fruitless prayer:
I, their pride and wealth disdaining
　　Should my humble hopes prevail,
Happy then, would cease complaining,
　　Blest with Patty of the Vale.

SAD WAS THE DAY

SAD was the day when my Willy did leave me,
　　Sad were the moments that wing'd him away;
And oh, most distressing, and most it did grieve me,
　　To witness his looks while I begg'd him to stay.

It hurt him to think that in vain was I crying,
　　Which I couldn't help, though I knew it so too;
The trumpets all sounding, the colours all flying,
　　A soldier my Willy—my Willy must go.

The youths, never heeding to-morrow and danger,
　　Kept laughing and toasting their girls o'er their beer;
But oh, my poor Willy, just like a lost stranger,
　　Stood speechless among them, half dead as it were.

He kiss'd me—'twas all—not a word when he started,
　　And oh, in his silence too much I could see,
He knew for a truth, and he knew, broken hearted,
　　That kiss was the last he should ever give me.

TO-DAY THE FOX MUST DIE: A HUNTING SONG

THE cock awakes the rosy dawn,
　　And tells approaching day,
While Reynard sneaks along the lawn

Belated with his prey:
Oh never think to find thy home,
    But for thy safety fly;
The sportsman's long proclaim'd thy doom,
    "To-day a Fox shall die."

The bugle blows, the sporting train
    Swift mount the snorting steed,
Each fence defiance bids in vain
    Their progress to impede;
The cover broke, they drive along,
    And raise a jovial cry;
Each dog barks chorus to my song,
    "To-day a Fox shall die."

Like lightning o'er the hills they sweep,
    The readiest roads they go;
The five-barr'd gate with ease they leap:
    Hark forward, tally ho!
The mist hangs on, and scents him strong,
    The moisture makes it lie;
The woods re-echo to my song,
    "This day the Fox must die."

Old Reynard finding shifts in vain,
    While hounds and horns pursue,
Now leaves the woods to try the plain,
    The bugle sounds a view:
Old Threadbrake gaily leads the throng;
    His bold unerring cry
Confirms the burthen of my song,
    "This day a Fox shall die."

His funeral knell the bugle blows,
    His end approaches near,
He reels and staggers as he goes,
    And drops his brush with fear:
More eager now they press along,
    And louder still the cry,

All join in chorus to my song,
  "To-day the Fox must die."

MY LAST SHILLING

O DISMAL disaster! O troublesome lot!
What a heart-rending theme for my musing I've got:
Then pray what's the matter?—O friend, I'm not willing,
      The thought grieves me sore,
      Now I'm driven to shore—
And must I then spend my last shilling, last shilling?
And must I then spend my last shilling?

O painful reflection! thou whole of my store,
That for these three months in my breeches I wore;
To spend thee, to spend thee, the thought turns me chilling:
      Oh, must I in spite
      Of all reason, this night,
A farewell bid to my last shilling, last shilling,
A farewell bid to my last shilling.

How oft in my corner I've bother'd my pate,
First mourn'd at my shilling, and then at my fate,
To think the world's riches—though painful and killing,
      While I here endure
      The sad pain past a cure,
Of being drain'd to my very last shilling, last shilling,
Of being drain'd to my very last shilling.

O couldst thou but answer, dear whole of my store,
I'd ask thee a question: Thus friendless and poor,
      Or whether it still
      Would be more to thy will
To stay, and be call'd my last shilling, last shilling?
To stay, and be call'd my last shilling?

Thou source of reflection, my friend, and my all!
For tho' I'm left friendless thou stick'st to thy stall;
And through each vexing trouble seem'st cheery and willing:

Thee to keep I'll contrive,
For I'm sure I shan't thrive
If ever I spend such a shilling, a shilling,
If ever I spend such a shilling.

So still, old companion, stick true to the breeches,
And wear this old pocket thread-bare to its stitches;
For ever to keep thee I really am willing:
And who knows, but what thou
(Though I'm hard ashore now)
May turn out a lucky last shilling, last shilling,
May turn out a lucky last shilling?

HER I LOVE

ROSE, in full blown blushes dyed,
Pink, maturely spread,
Carnations, boasting all their pride
Of melting white and red,
Are charms confess'd by every eye;
But, ah! how faint they prove
To paint superior charms, when nigh
The cheek of her I love.

Ripe cherry on its parent tree,
With full perfection grac'd,
Red coral in its native sea,
To all advantage plac'd;
What charms they boast the eye to please,
And beauty to improve:
But, ah! all's lost, when match'd with these
The lips of her I love.

The pulpy plum, when ripeness swells
Its down-surrounding blue—
The dews besprent on heather-bells,
Reflecting brighter hue—
The azure sky, when stars appear

Its blueness to improve,
Fade into dullest shades, when near
The eyes of her I love.

Sweet is the blossom'd bean's perfume,
By morning breezes shed;
And sweeter still the jonquil's bloom,
When eve bedews its head;
The perfume sweet of pink and rose,
And violet of the grove:
But ah! how sweeter far than those,
The kiss of her I love.

MY LOVE, THOU ART A NOSEGAY SWEET

MY love, thou art a nosegay sweet,
My sweetest flower I prove thee;
And pleas'd I pin thee to my breast,
And dearly do I love thee.

And when, my nosegay, thou shalt fade,
As sweet a flower thou'lt prove thee;
And as thou witherest on my breast,
For beauty past I'll love thee.

And when, my nosegay, thou shalt die,
And heaven's flower shalt prove thee;
My hopes shall follow to the sky,
And everlasting love thee.

MY LOVE'S LIKE A LILY

MY love's like a lily, my love's like a rose,
My love's like a smile the Spring mornings disclose;
And sweet as the rose, on her cheek her love glows,
When sweetly she smileth on me:

But as cold as the snow of the lily, my rose
Behaves to pretenders, whoever they be;

In vain higher stations their passions disclose,
    To win her affections from me.

My love's like a lily, my love's like a rose,
My love's like the smile the Spring mornings disclose;
And fair as the lily, and sweet as the rose,
    My love's beauty bloometh to me:
And smiles of more pleasure my heart only knows,
    To think that pretenders, whoever they be,
But vainly their love and their passions disclose;
    My love remains constant to me.

TRUE LOVE

TRUE love, the virgin's first fond passion,
    How blest the swain to prove it!
Should Hymen snatch the lucky hour,
    No power on earth can move it.

When death such loving hearts divides,
    And love on earth is blasting;
Firm fix'd the hope in heaven remains,
    Where love is everlasting.

THE FIRST OF MAY: A BALLAD

FAIR blooms the rose upon the green,
    Pretending to excel;
But who another rose has seen,
    A different tale can tell.
The morning smiles, the lark's begun
    To welcome in the May:
Be cloudless, skies! look out, bright sun!
    And haste my love away.

Though graceful round the maidens move,
    That join the rural ball,
Soon shall they own my absent love
    The rival of them all.

Go, wake your shepherdess, ye lambs!
    And murmur her delay:
Chide her neglect, ye hoarser dams!
    And call my love away.

Ye happy swains, with each a bride,
    Were but the angel there,
While slighted maids despair'd and sigh'd,
    You'd court th' unequall'd fair.
Dry up, ye dews! nor threat'ning hing,
    To soil her best array:
Ye birds! with double vigour sing,
    And urge my love away.

Welcome, sun! the dews are fled,
    The lark has rais'd his song;
The daisy nauntles up its head,—
    Why waits my love so long?
As flowrets fade, the pleasures bloom,
    All hastening to decay:
The day steals on, and showers may come:
    This instant haste away.

What now, ye fearful cringing sheep!
    Who meets your wondering eyes?
What makes you 'neath the maples creep,
    In homaging surprise?
No ladies tread our humble green:
    Ah! welcome wonders, hail!
I witness your mistaken queen
    Is Patty of the Vale.

SONNETS

THE SETTING SUN

THIS scene, how beauteous to a musing mind,
  That now swift slides from my enchanted view;
The Sun sweet setting yon far hills behind,
  In other worlds his visits to renew:
What spangled glories all around him shine;
  What nameless colours, cloudless and serene,
(A heav'nly prospect, brightest in decline,)
  Attend his exit from this lovely scene.
So sets the Christian's sun, in glories clear;
So shines his soul at his departure here:
  No clouding doubts, nor misty fears arise,
To dim Hope's golden rays of being forgiven;
  His Sun, sweet setting in the clearest skies,
In Faith's assurance wings the soul to heaven.

THE PRIMROSE

WELCOME, pale Primrose! starting up between
  Dead matted leaves of ash and oak, that strew
  The every lawn, the wood, and spinney through,
Mid creeping moss and ivy's darker green;
  How much thy presence beautifies the ground:
How sweet thy modest, unaffected pride
Glows on the sunny bank, and wood's warm side.
  And where thy fairy flowers in groups are found,
The school-boy roams enchantedly along,
  Plucking the fairest with a rude delight:
While the meek shepherd stops his simple song,
  To gaze a moment on the pleasing sight;
O'erjoy'd to see the flowers that truly bring
The welcome news of sweet returning Spring.

CHRISTIAN FAITH

WHAT antidote or charm on earth is found,
　To alleviate or soften fate's decree?
To fearless enter on that dark profound,
　Where life emerges in eternity?

Wisdom, a rushlight vainly boasting power
　To cheer the terrors Sin's first visit gave,
Denies existence at that dreadful hour,
　And shrinks in horror from a gaping grave.

O Christianity, thou charm divine!
That firmness, faith, and last resource is thine:
　With thee the Christian joys to lose his breath,
Nor dreads to find his mortal strength decay;
　But, dear in friendship, shakes the hand of Death,
And hugs the pain that gnaws his life away.

THE MOON

HOW sweet the Moon extends her cheering ray
　To damp the terrors of the darksome night,
Guiding the lonely traveller on his way,
　Pointing the path that leads his journey right.
　Hail! welcome! blessing! to thy silver light,
That charms dull night, and makes its horrors gay.
　So shines the Gospel to the Christian's soul;
So, by its light and inspiration given,
　He (spite of sin and Satan's black control)
Through all obstructions steers his course to heaven.
　So did the Saviour his design pursue,
That we, unworthy sinners, might be bless'd;
　So suffer'd death, its terrors to subdue,
And made the grave a wish'd-for place of rest.

THE GIPSY'S EVENING BLAZE

TO me how wildly pleasing is that scene
  Which doth present, in evening's dusky hour,
A group of Gipsies, centred on the green,
  In some warm nook where Boreas has no pow'r;
Where sudden starts the quivering blaze behind
  Short, shrubby bushes, nibbled by the sheep,
  That mostly on these short sward pastures keep;
Now lost, now seen, now bending with the wind:
And now the swarthy Sybil kneels reclin'd;
  With proggling stick she still renews the blaze,
  Forcing bright sparks to twinkle from the flaze.
When this I view, the all-attentive mind
  Will oft exclaim (so strong the scene pervades),
  "Grant me this life, thou Spirit of the Shades!"

A SCENE

THE Landscape's stretching view, that opens wide,
  With dribbling brooks, and river's wider floods,
  And hills, and vales, and darksome lowering woods,
With green of varied hues, and grasses pied;
  The low brown cottage in the shelter'd nook;
The steeple, peeping just above the trees
Whose dangling leaves keep rustling in the breeze;
  And thoughtful shepherd bending o'er his hook;
And maidens stripp'd, haymaking too, appear;
  And Hodge a whistling at his fallow plough;
  And herdsman hallooing to intruding cow:
All these, with hundreds more, far off and near,
  Approach my sight; and please to such excess,
  That language fails the pleasure to express.

TO THE GLOW-WORM

TASTEFUL Illumination of the night,
  Bright scatter'd, twinkling star of spangled earth!
Hail to the nameless colour'd dark-and-light,
  The witching nurse of thy illumin'd birth.
In thy still hour how dearly I delight
  To rest my weary bones, from labour free;
In lone spots, out of hearing, out of sight,
  To sigh day's smother'd pains; and pause on thee,
  Bedecking dangling brier and ivied tree,
Or diamonds tipping on the grassy spear;
  Thy pale-fac'd glimmering light I love to see,
Gilding and glistering in the dew-drop near:
  O still-hour's mate! my easing heart sobs free,
While tiny bents low bend with many an added tear.

THE ANT

THOU little Insect, infinitely small
  What curious texture marks thy minute frame!
How seeming large thy foresight, and withal,
  Thy labouring talents not unworthy fame,
To raise such monstrous hills along the plain,
  Larger than mountains, when compar'd with thee:
To drag the crumb dropp'd by the village swain,
  Huge size to thine, is strange, indeed, to me.
But that great Instinct which foretels the cold,
  And bids to guard 'gainst winter's wasteful power,
Endues this mite with cheerfulness to hold
  Its toiling labours through the sultry hour:
So that same soothing power, in misery,
Cheers the poor Pilgrim to Eternity.

TO HOPE

AH, smiling cherub! cheating Hope, adieu!
   No more I'll listen to your pleasing themes;
No more your flattering scenes with joy renew,
   For ah, I've found them all delusive dreams:
Yes, mere delusions all; therefore, adieu!
   No more shall you this aching heart beguile;
No more your fleeting joys will I pursue,
   That mock'd my sorrows when they seem'd to smile,
And flatter'd tales that never will be true:
   Tales, only told to aggravate distress
And make me at my fate the more repine,
   By whispering joys I never can possess,
And painting scenes that never can be mine.

A WINTER SCENE

HAIL, Scenes of desolation and despair,
   Keen Winter's overbearing sport and scorn!
Torn by his rage, in ruins as you are,
   To me more pleasing than a Summer's morn
Your shatter'd state appears;—despoil'd and bare,
   Stripp'd of your clothing, naked and forlorn:—
Yes, Winter's havock! wretched as you shine,
   Dismal to others as your fate may seem,
Your fate is pleasing to this heart of mine,
   Your wildest horrors I the most esteem.
The ice-bound floods that still with rigour freeze,
   The snow-cloth'd valley, and the naked tree,
These sympathising scenes my heart can please,
   Distress is their's—and they resemble me.

EVENING

NOW glaring daylight's usher'd to a close;
  And nursing Eve her soothing care renews,
To welcome weary labour to repose,
  And cherish nature with reviving dews.
Hail, cooling sweets! that breathe so sweetly here;
  Hail, lovely Eve! whose hours so lovely prove;
Thy silent calm! to solitude so dear;
  And oh, this darkness! dearer still to love.
Now the fond lover seeks thy silent plains,
  And with his charmer in fond dalliance strays,
Vowing his love, and telling jealous pains
  Which doubtful fancies in their absence raise.
Ah! though such pleasures centre not in me,
I love to wander and converse with thee.

TO THE WINDS

HAIL, gentle Winds! I love your murmuring sound;
  The willows charm me, wavering to and fro;
And oft I stretch me on the daisied ground,
  To see you crimp the wrinkled flood below:
Delighted more as brisker gusts succeed,
  And give the landscape round a sweeter grace,
Sweeping in shaded waves the ripening mead,
  Puffing their rifled fragrance in my face.
Painters of Nature! ye are doubly dear;
  Her children dearly love your whispering charms:
Ah, ye have murmur'd sweet to many an ear
  That now lies dormant in Death's icy arms;
And at this moment many a weed ye wave,
That hides the Bard in his forgotten grave.

NATIVE SCENES

O NATIVE Scenes, for ever, ever dear!
　So blest, so happy as I here have been,
　So charm'd with nature in each varied scene,
To leave you all is cutting and severe.
　Ye hawthorn bushes that from winds would screen,
Where oft I've shelter'd from a threaten'd shower,
In youth's past bliss, in childhood's happy hour,
　Ye woods I've wandered, seeking out the nest;
Ye meadows gay that rear'd me many a flower,
　Where, pulling cowslips, I've been doubly blest,
Humming gay fancies as I pluck'd the prize:
　Oh, fate unkind! beloved Scenes, adieu!
Your vanish'd pleasures crowd my swimming eyes,
　And make the wounded heart to bleed anew.

TO A FAVOURITE TREE

OLD, favourite Tree! art thou too fled the scene?
　Could not thy 'clining age the axe delay,
And let thee stretch thy shadows o'er the green,
　And let thee die in picturesque decay?
What hadst thou done to meet a tyrant's frown?
　Small value was the ground on which thou stood;
But gain's rude rage it was that cut thee down,
　And dragg'd thee captive from thy native wood.
So gay in summer as thy boughs were dress'd,
　So soft, so cool, as then thy leaves did wave;
I knew thee then, and knowing am distress'd:
　And like as Friendship leaning o'er the grave,
Loving you all, ye trees, ye bushes, dear,
I wander where ye stood, and shed my bosom-tear.

APPROACH OF SPRING

SWEET are the omens of approaching Spring,
　When gay the elder sprouts her winged leaves;
When tootling robins carol-welcomes sing,
　And sparrows chelp glad tidings from the eaves.
What lovely prospects wait each wakening hour,
　When each new day some novelty displays;
How sweet the sun-beam melts the crocus flower,
　Whose borrow'd pride shines dizen'd in his rays:
Sweet, new-laid hedges flush their tender greens;
Sweet peep the arum-leaves their shelter screens;
　Ah! sweet is all which I'm denied to share:
Want's painful hindrance sticks me to her stall;—
　But still Hope's smiles unpoint the thorns of Care,
Since Heaven's eternal Spring is free for all.

SUMMER

THE oak's slow-opening leaf, of deepening hue,
　Bespeaks the power of Summer once again;
While many a flower unfolds its charms to view,
　To glad the entrance of his sultry reign.
Where peep the gaping, speckled cuckoo-flowers,
　Sweet is each rural scene she brings to pass;
Prizes to rambling school-boys' vacant hours,
　Tracking wild searches through the meadow grass:
The meadow-sweet taunts high its showy wreath,
And sweet the quaking grasses hide beneath.
　Ah, 'barr'd from all that sweetens life below,
Another Summer still my eyes can see
　Freed from the scorn and pilgrimage of woe,
To share the Seasons of Eternity.

THE RIVER GWASH

WHERE winding Gwash whirls round its wildest scene,
    On this romantic bend I sit me down;
On that side view the meadow's smoothing green,
    Edg'd with the peeping hamlet's checquering brown;
    Here the steep bank, as dropping headlong down;
While glides the stream a silver streak between,
    As glide the shaded clouds along the sky,
Bright'ning and deep'ning, losing as they're seen,
In light and shade: to where old willows lean,
    Thus their broad shadow runs the river by,
With tree and bush replete, a wilder'd scene,
    And moss and ivy speckling on my eye.
Oh, thus while musing wild, I'm doubly blest,
My woes unheeding, and my heart at rest.

TO RELIGION

THOU sacred light, that right from wrong discerns;
    Thou safeguard of the soul, thou heaven on earth;
Thou undervaluer of the world's concerns,
    Thou disregarder of its joys and mirth;
Thou only home the houseless wanderers have;
    Thou prop by which the pilgrim's woes are borne;
Thou solace of the lonely hermit's cave,
    That beds him down to rest on fate's sharp thorn;
Thou only hope to sorrow's bosom given;
    Thou voice of mercy when the weary call;
Thou faith extending to thy home in heaven;
    Thou peace, thou rest, thou comfort, all in all:
O sovereign good! on thee all hopes depend,
Till thy grand source unfolds its realizing end.

ANXIETY

ONE, o'er heaths wandering in a pitch dark night,
　　Making to sounds that hope some village near;
Hermit, retreating to a chinky light,
　　Long lost in winding cavern dark and drear;
　　A slave, long banish'd from his country dear,
By freedom left to seek his native plains;
　　A soldier, absent many a long, long year,
In sight of home ere he that comfort gains;
A thirsty labouring wight, that wistful strains
　　O'er the steep hanging bank to reach the stream;
A hope, delay so lingeringly detains,
　　We still on point of its disclosure seem:
These pictures weakly 'semble to the eye
A *faint* existence of Anxiety.

EXPECTATION

WHEN Expectation in the bosom heaves,
　　What longing, anxious views disturb the mind;
What fears, what hopes, distrust and then believe
　　That something which the heart expects to find!
How the poor prisoner, ere he's doom'd to die,
　　Within his gloomy cell of dreary woe,
How does he watch, with Expectation's eye,
　　The lingering, long suspense of fate to know.
Alas, poor soul! though different bonds confine;
The walls his prison is, the world is mine:
　　So do I turn my weary eyes above,
So do I look and sigh for peace to come,
　　So do I long the grave's dark end to prove,
And anxious wait my long, long journey home.

TO MY OATEN REED

THOU Warble wild, of rough, rude melody!
　　How oft I've woo'd thee, often thrown thee by;
In many a doubtful rapture touching thee,
　　Waking thy rural notes in many a sigh:
　　Fearing the wise, the wealthy, proud and high,
Would scorn as vain thy lowly extasy;
　　Deeming presumptuous thy uncultur'd themes.
Thus vainly courting Taste's unblemish'd eye,
　　To list a simple Labourer's artless dreams,
　　Haply I wander into wide extremes.
But O thou sweet, wild-winding rhapsody,
　　Thou jingling charm that dost my heart control;
I take thee up to smother many a sigh,
　　And lull the throbbings of a woe-worn soul.

THE COUNTRY GIRL

OH, dear! what fine thinkings beset me,
Since the young farmer yesterday met me,
To tell me for truth he would get me
   Some service more fitting in town:
For he said 'twas a shame, and he swore too,
That I should be serv'd so and more too,
And that he was vex'd o'er and o'er too,
   To see me so sadly run down.

When to thank him, for curtsey'ng I dropp'd me,
He said 'twas all foolish, and stopp'd me;
And into his arms, oh! he popp'd me,
   And crumpled my bonnet awry:
The tray sav'd the fall, till he mov'd it,
And this way and that way he shov'd it;
Good behaviour, he said, how he lov'd it,
   When maids were not foolish and shy.

Oh dear! what fine thinkings beset me,
Since the young farmer promis'd, and met me,
Of what he would do and would get me,
   How my heart pittipatters about:
Though fear—none but fools make a trade on—
He swore when he saw what I play'd on,
"My word is my bond, pretty maiden!"
   Then why need I harbour a doubt?

Though the tale-clacking grass's foul staining
In my holiday clothes is remaining,
I ne'er shall go make a complaining,
   I've promise of better in town:
So Chub needn't come again croaking,
To maul one about, so provoking,
I know what is what, without joking,
   There's nought got by pleasing a clown.

22063217R00060

Printed in Poland
by Amazon Fulfillment
Poland Sp. z o.o., Wrocław